God Is Green

Ecology for Christians

IAN BRADLEY

Foreword by Jonathon Porritt

IMAGE BOOKS
DOUBLEDAY
New York London Toronto Sydney Auckland

AN IMAGE BOOK
PUBLISHED BY DOUBLEDAY
a division of Bantam Doubleday Dell Publishing Group, Inc.
666 Fifth Avenue, New York, New York 10103

IMAGE and DOUBLEDAY are trademarks of Doubleday,
a division of Bantam Doubleday Dell Publishing Group, Inc.

This Image Books edition published March 1992 by special
arrangement with Darton, Longman and Todd Ltd.

Library of Congress Cataloging-in-Publication Data

Bradley, Ian C.
God is green : ecology for Christians / Ian
Bradley ; foreword by Jonathon Porritt.
p.   cm.
Includes bibliographical references.
1. Nature—Religious aspects—Christianity.
2. Human ecology—Religious aspects—Christianity.
3. Man—Influence on nature.
I. Title.
BT695.5.B72   1992
231.7—dc20   91-35599
CIP

ISBN 0-385-42279-2

Contents

Foreword

I distinctly recall a public meeting in Durham, around the time of the 1983 General Election, when I was called upon to speculate about the political leanings of Christ. 'In the event of a Second Coming', intoned a lugubrious looking man in the back row, 'do you not agree that the Son of God would almost certainly vote Green, in that it is only a green philosophy which both reveres God's Earth *and* endeavours to put the Sermon on the Mount into practice?'

My very limited grasp of theology left me ill-equipped to deal with this spiritual green googly, and I suspect that my answer was less than enlightening. There are, anyway, too many people who nonchalantly conscript the dead and buried (and even the resurrected) into their own paper armies, with little intellectual justification, and even less integrity.

But I have pondered this encounter on and off since then, and have become increasingly convinced that the real question is not so much whether or not Christ would vote Green, but whether or not the Church would have him declared a heretic for so doing!

In any objective analysis of the root causes of today's ecological crisis, there are many who still incline the opinion that the Christian Church has always been (and still is) part of the problem rather than part of the solution. They feel this despite the fact that many thousands of Christians have been in the vanguard, as individuals, in befriending and defending the Earth. As a somewhat wayward and unorthodox Christian myself, that ambivalence has caused me no little pain over the years.

So when I heard that Ian Bradley (whom I have known

for a long time as a teacher and astute observer of the political scene) had not only become a Minister in the Church of Scotland, but was bringing out a book entitled *God is Green*, my spirits soared in eager anticipation. Never again would I be floored on the hypothetical voting intentions of any one element of the Trinity!

My expectations have not been disappointed. I have no doubt that the academic theologians will have a fine old time of it, debating some of the finer points of exegesis, but essentially this is a book written for the ordinary but interested lay-persons, for the pew-fillers and the hymn-singers, and for those keen to learn more about the origins and meaning of their faith without being pinioned within this or that dogmatic straitjacket.

I have learned much from this book. It has allowed me to rethink some of my rather superficial criticism of the anti-ecological practice and preaching of the Christian Church. It has given words to some of my own inchoate feelings about creation and God's continuously shaping hand in the process of evolution. And it has reinforced me in my belief that the Green Movement is never likely to move very far at all if it remains bogged down in its current state of secular, anthropocentric sterility.

If it is the destiny of this generation to become stewards of God's Earth (and it had better be, for we are the last generation likely to be given such a choice), then Christianity is going to have to be comprehensively reinterpreted and its long-suppressed sacramental vision sung out anew. We do not, as Ian quite rightly argues, need to invent a new religion; but Christianity assuredly needs to rediscover some of its own very old and resolutely earth-bound wisdom.

Beneath all the scholarship and sensitive interpretation, this book is really a paean of praise to the living Earth. By a happy coincidence, I have been reading it during a brief but gloriously revitalising visit to the Lake District. Stick anybody on the top of Wansdyke Fell, on a crisp October evening, with the whole of Lake Windermere caught momentarily in a final surge of sunlight, and I defy them at such a moment in such a place not to find a sense of transcendent purpose and a stirring intimation of God.

The Green Movement is very much in the news these days. It is a young, confident, and increasingly influential movement, but it plays a dangerous game with those who are driving humankind to the edge of an ecological abyss. Those who should know better have seized on ideas like 'green consumerism' as if they promise salvation without any sacrifice – or even any real change. It will not be so easy as that, and the Green Movement will not sustain itself, let alone learn to sustain indefinitely the life-support systems on which we and all future generations depend, unless it finds a deeper set of values. One cannot sustain that which one does not revere.

This book will add great weight to the Green Movement's coming of age, and will have enlightened and inspired not a few of us in the process.

JONATHON PORRITT

Lake District
October 1989

Preface

This book really grew out of an article in the *Guardian's* 'Face to Faith' column in November 1988 in which I argued for a 'greening' of Christianity. It evoked a greater response than anything else I have written over nearly twenty years in full-time or freelance journalism. Indeed I am still receiving letters from people who read it. This encouraged me to develop my thought on the subject, and all who communicated with me about the article must share some of the credit (or the blame) for the present volume.

I could never have embarked on a work like this, however popular and superficial its theological content, without the solid academic grounding that I have received over the last three years in the course of studying for a Bachelor of Divinity degree at St Andrews University. My tutors there have nobly put up with a rather argumentative and awkward student. To four in particular I owe a special debt of gratitude: Professor Bill Shaw introduced me to the exciting subject of process thought and to the whole area of creation theology; Michael Keeling took me on a fascinating and very rewarding journey of discovery through the world of Christian mysticism and spirituality which took in such leading exponents of Green Christianity as St Francis of Assisi and Dame Julian of Norwich; Steven Mackie encouraged my interest in ecology and land reform and Dr Ron Piper allowed me to develop my rather idiosyncratic theories about the meaning of the nature miracles in the New Testament and also stressed the theme of God's sustaining care for all his creation that comes across in Jesus' wisdom teaching.

My developing thoughts on the intrinsic greenness of Christianity have been inflicted on a number of Church of Scotland congregations in Dundee and North-East Fife. They have received what must often have come as strange and unorthodox sermons with patience and in many cases with encouraging enthusiasm. I have relied heavily on the published work of a number of contemporary theologians, especially Dr A. R. Peacocke, Dr John Polkinghorne, Professor Jürgen Moltmann, Professor George Hendry and Metropolitan Paulos Gregorios. My debt to them will, I hope, be clear from the text. I am very grateful to the Revd Francis Simons, minister at Essex Unitarian Church in London, for permission to quote his poem 'To plant a tree', and to Wild Goose Publications for permission to quote from George MacLeod's prayer 'The whole earth shall cry glory'. Biblical quotations are from the Revised Standard Version, unless otherwise indicated.

I would also like to thank Sarah Baird-Smith and others at Darton Longman & Todd. It is, I think, appropriate that this book should be coming out under the imprint of a publishing house which produces a large number of Roman Catholic books. Although I write as a Protestant minister I am deeply conscious of the enormously Green and holistic side to the whole Roman Catholic tradition. I am also conscious of that pertinent question posed by Simone Weil: 'How can the church call itself Catholic if the universe itself is left out?'

My wife Lucy has, as always, cheerfully put up with my frequent disappearances to my study and steered the children out of my way during the composition of yet another book. I hope she will forgive me if I dedicate this volume not just to her but to all those who were schooled in the sixties and who will be reaching their half century on the planet earth around the year 2000 – the generation of Prince Charles and Jonathon Porritt, both of whom have been an inspiration to me as I know they have to many others.

IAN BRADLEY

Introduction

There can be little doubt that the threat posed by human exploitation and pollution of the natural environment is the most serious problem facing the world as we enter the last decade of the twentieth century. The scale of the ecological crisis is enormous and rising all the time – but so too is the extent of human concern about it. The battle to save the environment has captured the hearts and imaginations of millions of people, not just those who vote for the Greens or join Friends of the Earth. It is now firmly on the mainstream political and social agenda and can no longer be dismissed as a fringe issue of interest only to cranks and faddists.

This book seeks to show that the Christian faith is intrinsically Green, that the good news of the Gospel promises liberation and fulfilment for the whole of creation and that Christians have a positive and distinctive contribution to make to the salvation of our threatened planet and the preservation of the natural environment. But in order to find this Green gospel at the heart of Christianity we need to clear away centuries of anthropocentric thinking which has put man rather than God at the centre of the universe and which has made the Church in the western world at least one of the prime aiders and abetters of the exploitation and pollution of the earth's resources.

The Christian religion has a bad name among many in the Green movement. Perhaps the most trenchant modern attack on the damage that it has done was made in 1967 in an article entitled 'The historical roots of our ecologic crisis' in the American magazine *Science*. It has almost attained the status of a classic text and is frequently quoted by those concerned about what is happening to the environment. The author, Professor Lynn White, argues forcefully that Christian arrogance towards nature lies at the root of many of our present troubles. More precisely he sees the Judaeo–Christian tradition as paving the way for human exploitation of nature by overthrowing the animism of pagan religions and introducing a new axiom – that nature has no reason for existence save to serve the purposes of man:

> Especially in its Western form, Christianity is the most anthropocentric religion the world has seen. In absolute contrast to ancient paganism and Asia's religions, it not only established a dualism of man and nature but also insisted that it is God's will that man exploit nature for his proper ends.[1]

There is a good deal of justice in this argument. The western churches, particularly since the Reformation, have been almost totally anthropocentric in their teaching and have had virtually no regard for the non-human elements in God's creation. It is hardly surprising that many of those who in recent years have to come to care deeply about the world of animals, plants, rivers and mountains have turned to eastern religions or gone back to old pagan beliefs for spiritual succour and inspiration. Certainly on the face of it Buddhism, Hinduism and Taoism, or the worship of Mother Earth, would seem much more congenial faiths for an environmentally conscious person to espouse than Christianity.

Nor can one blame many of those who are now seeking a new set of values to govern the relationship between humans and nature for writing off Christianity as a possible source for a new ecological ethic. A leading article in the *New Scientist* in 1970 argued that it was no use looking to Christianity for the new value system which the West desperately needs and in which 'man regards the soil as a partner to be cherished rather than as a captive to be raped'. Rather it felt 'we need to turn to Hindu or Buddhist faiths . . . or the peasant cultures of Asia'.[2] In his thoughtful book *Man's Responsibility for Nature*, published in 1980, John Passmore writes that Christian theology cannot give itself a genuinely Green hue without ceasing to be distinctively Christian and giving up its sense of man's metaphysical uniqueness.

But is the call for human exploitation and domination of nature that many people have discerned in Christianity a true reflection of the faith or rather a gross distortion of its central message? There are three elements of traditional Christian doctrine which have rightly been identified as major contributors to the environmental crisis which we now face. The first is the idea that nature exists solely for man's benefit, which is derived from God's command to Adam in the opening chapter of the Bible to have dominion over the rest of creation. The second is the image of God encouraged by attempts to distance Christianity from pantheistic pagan cults which tends to portray a wholly transcendent Deity totally separated from the world which he created and with no continuing interest or involvement in its non-human elements. The third is the notion of the natural world as a sphere of profanity and darkness, which derives both from traditional dualistic distinctions between matter and spirit and from the specific doctrine of the fall.

In the first three chapters I seek to show that each of these teachings represents both a total distortion of the original meaning of the biblical texts from which it has been derived and a reversal of the teachings of the early Church. More positively, I will be arguing that far from having a negative message about the world of nature Christianity is in fact the most concerned of all the world's great religions about the fate of the non-human as well as the human part of creation. It alone speaks of God becoming incarnate in physical matter and sending his Son to be the cosmic Christ, the one who will redeem and lift up the whole world to the glory of the Father. This theme is the subject of Chapter 4. The fifth chapter explores the uniquely positive and creative role that Christianity envisages for human beings as stewards, artists, mediators, priests and redeemers of the world, in which they live as fellow-sufferers with the host of other creatures, animate and inanimate, with which God has filled the earth. I end with some suggestions about how the churches might themselves become greener in response to this central, if long neglected, strain in the faith which they profess.

I do not claim any great originality for my main argument. One of the most encouraging features of Christian theology over the last two decades or so has been a turning away from the narrowly anthropocentric themes of individual salvation, justification and atonement that have preoccupied churches in the West for so long, towards a more universal and cosmic approach. A welcome consequence of this shift in emphasis has been a much greater stress on the doctrine of creation, seen as a major theme in its own right and not just as a prelude to the arrival on the scene of the two giants of sin and salvation. A leading proponent of this new creation-centred theology has been Claus Westermann, one of the leading Old Testament scholars of this century. His castigation of the narrow anthropocentrism that has bedevilled so much western theology over the last four centuries or more sounds a clarion call for a new more ecological approach:

> When the theology and the preaching of the Church are concerned only with salvation, when God's dealing with man is limited to the forgiveness of sins or to justification, the necessary consequence is that it is only in this context that man has to deal with God and God with man. This means that God is not concerned with a worm being trodden to the earth or with the appearance of a new star in the Milky Way. And so the question must be put: what sort of God is he who does everything for the salvation of man but clearly has nothing at all to do with man in his life situation.[3]

It is sadly the case that some of the most influential movements in contemporary theology continue to cling to the besetting sin of anthropocentrism. This is certainly true of the existentialist approach pioneered by Rudolf Bultmann which presents the Christian Gospel in largely psychological terms as an answer and a challenge to individual human beings in their particular predicaments and not as a message of good news for the whole cosmos. It is true too of much of the liberation theology which has made so much headway in the Third World and is now radicalising Christians in the West. Although the theologians of liberation have done much to break down the individualism of traditional Christianity by stressing the category of community, they have largely confined their attention to the human race and have little to say about the liberation of the rest of struggling creation.

Certain other contemporary movements both within and outside the churches, however, are at last rejecting anthropocentric themes in favour of a much more holistic and cosmic approach. The feminist movement has rightly identified male supremacy as lying behind many of our religious images and teachings. It has planted a big question mark over the classical theistic picture of God as a remote patriarchal figure in the sky and returned to a much more biblical sense of the Creator which stresses such attributes as tenderness and loving care and picks up images of maternity and fertility from the medieval mystics. Process thought, almost certainly the most stimulating and suggestive movement in contemporary theology, finally rids us of the classical Greek influences which have caused the Christian God to be seen as omnipotent, absolute and unchanging. Instead it stresses the dynamism which is such a feature of the Old Testament picture of the Creator, and builds on it to suggest that God is in fact supremely flexible, fluid, relative and constantly changing and active throughout his creation, which he animates by persuasion and creating possibilities rather than brute force and coercion – in A. N. Whitehead's memorable phrase, 'the poet of the world, luring it by his vision of truth, beauty and goodness'.

Both feminism and process theology are undoubtedly helping to reverse the anthropocentric tide that has flowed through Christianity for so long. Restoration of the idea of a God who is concerned with the totality of his creation and not just with human beings is also being helped by the activities and perceptions of scientists, especially those working in the fields of biology and quantum physics. Increasingly scientists are using religious or at least poetic language to express their awe and wonder at the beautiful, intricate and mysterious world that they are discovering at the sub-atomic level. The discovery of a unified field in physics and a phylogenetic field in biology suggest a deep unity and harmony at the root of all being. At the same time quantum physics has revealed the world to be much freer and more open than the deterministic machine pictured by Isaac Newton. No longer can God be seen as the remote watchmaker in the sky who has wound up the mechanism of the universe and observes from a distance as it ticks away. Modern science suggests rather a creator and sustainer of all things who is constantly active in the world, offering new possibilities to every part of his creation.

Spurred on both by these new developments in the intellectual field and by a growing recognition of the seriousness of the ecological crisis facing the world, the major churches in the West have taken a new interest in the long neglected theology of nature. There is strong agreement among them that the whole non-human world needs to be treated much more seriously and positively by Christianity. A Church of England working party on the subject as long ago as 1975 reported that 'what is needed is a religious world-picture which portrays a common order under which man and his fellow creatures live, and in which we can relate man, his work, and organic and inorganic nature to each other'.[4] The Church of Scotland's Religion, Science and Technology Unit produced a powerful ecological statement in 1986 under the title 'While the earth endures'. A series of papal encyclicals, beginning with Paul VI's *Octagesima Adveniens* in 1971 and culminating in John Paul II's *Solicitudo Rei Socialis* in 1988, have condemned human exploitation and pollution of natural resources and stressed the unity and interdependence of all creation.

On an international and inter-denominational level, the World Council of Churches has been vigorously pursuing a programme of working parties, conferences and publications based on the themes of justice, peace and the integrity of creation. A recent newsletter from the Central Council of the Church and Society Division points to the need for 'a credible theology of nature which takes into account the discoveries

6

and insights of biblical studies, science and dialogue with other religious traditions and ideologies'.[5] Goodness knows how many trees have been felled to produce the numerous papers, pamphlets and books that have come out in recent years calling for more environmental sensitivity and ecological awareness among the churches. And here I am adding to the pile, although at least this book is printed on environmentally friendly, non-dioxin bleached paper!

I have two particular reasons for writing this book. The first is to suggest that what we need is not, as is so often argued (including in some of the reports I have just mentioned), a new theology of nature but rather a return to the original message contained in the Bible and preached and practised in the early Church. If this book has one central theme it is that greening Christianity does not involve grafting on to it some alien philosophy but simply restoring its original character. Indeed, it means stripping off a whole series of alien layers that have accumulated to reveal the original greenness of the Garden of Eden and the cross on Calvary. Of course new movements like feminism and process thought and new scientific hypotheses like quantum physics and the Gaia thesis can help us restate the cosmic nature of Christianity in terms which are meaningful today. Our faith constantly needs to be re-expressed in the language and thought-forms of the day. But its essentials do not need to be changed.

Certainly in order to proclaim the greenness of Christianity we do not need any new doctrines or new theology. We need simply to return with a new eye and new attention to the Scriptures – to the prophets and psalmists of the Old Testament who proclaim God's continuing concern for all his creation; to the Gospel writers who portray Jesus as the man who communes with the wild beasts and who stills the storm; to St Paul who writes of the cosmic mission of Christ and who sums up the Christian approach to nature in that wonderful passage in his epistle to the Romans in which he portrays the whole created order groaning and in travail for its deliverance and liberation. We can find these same themes reflected and expanded in the writings of the early Church Fathers, in the lives of the great Celtic saints who brought the Gospel to our own lands and in the rich tradition of medieval spirituality and mysticism.

We can find the essential greenness of Christianity expressed too in the writings of many who have lived through that long period of anthropocentric and negative Christianity inaugurated by St Augustine, confirmed by the Reformation and from which we are only now beginning to emerge. In the following pages you will find extracts from poems, meditations, sermons and books by many who never lost their sense of the Green heart of Christianity when most around them, and certainly the mainstream churches, had. They held on to that idea expressed so well by Pierre Teilhard de Chardin 'that the world – the world beloved of God – has, even more than individuals, a soul to be redeemed'.[6] You will also find many references to the eastern Orthodox tradition which has so much to offer us in the West as we seek to recover a holistic and cosmic outlook.

There are many long-lost or neglected ideas and images from the past which can help us to recover Green Christianity. Many of them are explored here – the great chain of being, the dance of creation, the pleroma of fullness of God's creation, the cosmic Christ, the recapitulation of all things, the sacred nature of matter implied in the doctrines of the Incarnation and the Eucharist, the theme of the garden that runs through the Bible from Eden to Gethsemane. But perhaps above all we need to pray for the grace to see God as much through his works as through his words. The idea that God's wonder and his purposes are revealed to us through nature as well as through the Bible is one that we badly need to recover. It was put very clearly by Sir Francis Bacon in 1605 when he distinguished the book of God's words and the book of his works. But the principle of finding God through nature goes back much earlier than that – it is at the heart of the much-neglected Catholic doctrine of natural theology, which provides a tremendous corrective to anthropocentric tendencies by stressing reasons for belief in God far outside the human world. It is beautifully expressed in that simple and much-loved children's hymn 'All things bright and beautiful' and in John Keble's verses from *The Christian Year:*

There is a book who runs may read
  Which heavenly truth imparts,
And all the lore its scholars need,
  Pure eyes and Christian hearts.

The works of God above, below,
  Within us and around,
Are pages in that book, to show
  How God himself is found.

One word of qualification is perhaps as well at this point. Some readers may gain the impression that I am of the opinion that Christianity has little to do with human beings and almost everything to do with the non-human parts of creation. May I dispel this idea from the outset. Humans are portrayed in the Bible as the chief of God's creatures and the Gospels are clear that we should be concerned above all in this life for our fellow men and women. Nothing that I say should detract from Our Lord's second great commandment to us. Nor would I for a moment deny that it is through other human beings that we see most clearly God's loving purposes revealed through Christ. I am not suggesting that we adopt a kind of misanthropic mysticism which finds the divine only in nature and not in man. As I hope I make clear, Christians can have no truck with some of the more extreme deep ecologists, or dark Greens, to be found in the United States and very occasionally in Britain, who see humans as a blight on our planet and who worship wild nature. For Christians respect for nature comes as an adjunct to rather than a substitute for respect for humans. In seeking to restore the greenness of Christianity, my sentiments are those of Byron's *Childe Harold*: 'I love not man the less, but Nature more'.

In a recent article in *The Times* Clifford Longley, that stimulating commentator on the contemporary religious scene, observed that the 1980s had not thrown up one interesting, original or powerful religious idea. The sixties, he pointed out, spawned liberation theology and the seventies feminist theology but the eighties had been a barren decade.[7] I think there is a good case for saying that the last ten years has in fact seen the rebirth of Green Christianity. The literature on the subject has certainly been considerable in both quantity and quality. The renaissance could be said to have begun in 1978 with the publication by the World Council of Churches of Paulos Gregorios' *The Human Presence: towards an orthodox view of nature*. The following year saw the publication of A. R. Peacocke's important *Creation and the World of Science*, which gives an Anglican view of the integrity and sacramentalism of nature. George Hendry's highly stimulating *Theology of Nature* appeared in 1980. Among the most important books of the eighties have been Robert Faricy, *Wind and Sea Obey Him: approaches to a theology of nature* (1982); Matthew Fox, *Original Blessing* (1983); Jürgen Moltmann, *God in Creation: an ecological doctrine of creation* (1985); and Sean McDonagh's *To Care for the Earth: a call to a new theology* (1986). These works taken together seem to me to constitute a pretty formidable attempt to establish a powerful religious idea – the realisation that we belong to the world rather than that the world belongs to us.

Despite all that has come out in the last decade or so, the message does not seem to have reached congregations and individual church members. It is still rare to hear sermons or prayers dealing with Green themes. Many Christians remain stuck in the old anthropocentric rut of individual salvation, justification and atonement. That brings me to my second main reason for writing this book. It springs from an almost missionary urge to spread the Green gospel of Christianity and a conviction that, if the 1980s have been barren of religious ideas, the 1990s must be the decade of Green theology, put forward not as some aberrant departure but as the very core of our faith in the one God who is concerned with all his creation and in his Son, Jesus Christ, the redeemer of the cosmos.

Millions of people, particularly among the young, are desperately concerned and worried about what is happening to the natural environment. They are often the people who reject Christianity because it seems narrowly individualistic and obsessed with such unattractive concepts as sin and retribution. I believe that Christianity has something vital and positive to say about these worries, that it offers faith, hope and also a positive role to play in preserving and saving the environment. I am equally sure that if Christians fail to speak on what is almost certainly the most important issue of our time and do not enter into dialogue with those who are concerned about the environment, we will not only have lost an enormous missionary and pastoral opportunity but we will have failed the human race, the planet and, most important of all, we will have failed God; the Father who knows and cares about one sparrow falling from heaven, the Son who communed with and redeemed the wayward forces of nature and the Holy Spirit who broods over the face of the waters just as she moves within our souls.

1

God's concern for all creation
The earth is the Lord's and the fullness thereof

We need go no further than the end of the opening chapter of the Bible to find the statement that is often taken to lie at the root of human arrogance and indifference towards the world of nature and which has led many people to see Christianity as being responsible for our current environmental crisis:

> Then God said, 'Let us make man in our image, after our likeness; and let them have dominion over the fish of the sea, and over the birds of the air, and over the cattle, and over all the earth, and over every creeping thing that creeps upon the earth.' (Gen. 1:26)

The message of this well-known verse seems to be clear. Man is lord of all he surveys, given by God the right to do what he likes with the rest of creation which is there simply to satisfy his wants and to be used for his enjoyment. There is no doubt that the biblical creation story has often been interpreted by Christians in this way, particularly since the Reformation. John Calvin wrote in his great commentary on Genesis that 'the end for which all things were created (was) that none of the conveniences and necessaries of life might be wanting to men'.[1] The early pages of Keith Thomas' fascinating *Man and the Natural World* are filled with similar statements culled from the writings of sixteenth- and seventeenth-century divines. Ever more ingenious explanations were advanced to show how every single thing on earth existed simply for the benefit of human beings, however far-fetched it might seem. In the mid-seventeenth century, for example, Henry More argued that God had created garden weeds to exercise the industry of man to dig them out: 'Had he nothing to struggle with, the fire of his spirit would be half extinguished.'[2] Two hundred years later the Revd William Kirby argued that even the louse had its role, providing a powerful incentive to habits of personal cleanliness.

This kind of thinking has persisted well into the twentieth century. In 1930 John Dickie, Professor of Systematic Theology at Aberdeen University and Moderator of the General Assembly of the Church of Scotland, wrote:

> The world exists for our sakes and not for its own. That follows from the truth that it is only personal beings capable of responding to Love that can be objects of Love in the true meaning of the term. God wills the world therefore as a means, but only as a means.[3]

In 1963 another Church of Scotland minister defended his action in shooting two of Gavin Maxwell's adopted otter cubs as they were playing on the shore on the grounds that 'The Lord gave man control over the beasts of the field.'[4] This instrumental and anthropocentric attitude towards the rest of creation has not been confined to Protestants. It is deeply embedded in classical Roman Catholic theology, as expressed in St Thomas Aquinas' observation: 'If any passage in Holy Scripture seems to forbid us to be cruel to brute animals, that is either lest through being cruel to animals one becomes cruel to human beings or because injury to an animal leads to the temporal hurt of man.'[5] In similar vein John Henry Newman's article on animals in the *Catholic Encyclopaedia* includes the comment: 'We may use them, we may destroy them at our pleasure . . . for our own ends, for our own benefit or satisfaction.'[6]

There is no doubt that such interpretations of God's commission to man in Genesis have provided a warrant for human exploitation and destruction of nature. It is hardly surprising that many of those concerned about the environment have echoed the verdict of the Victorian poet Wilfred Scawen Blunt that Christianity is to blame for the 'atrocious doctrine that beasts and birds were made solely for man's pleasure and that he had no duties towards them'.[7] Robert Burns doubtless had the words of Genesis 1:26 in mind when he wrote his poem 'To a Mouse':

> I'm truly sorry man's dominion
> Has broken nature's social union,
> An' justifies the ill opinion
> Which makes thee startle
> At me, thy poor, earth-born companion,
> An' fellow-mortal!

But is human exploitation of nature really the message of the commission given to man in the Genesis creation story, or is it a complete distortion of the theme of God's concern for the totality of his creation that sounds throughout the Old Testament? I believe that the view of the relationship between humans and the rest of the world that we have derived from the Bible is at odds with the real message of the Scriptures. It is a consequence of our besetting sin as human beings, which is to be totally anthropocentric and to put man at the centre of the universe. I use the masculine form deliberately here as elsewhere: anthropocentrism is a peculiarly male sin, and not the least virtue of the contemporary feminist movement is that it is encouraging a more humble and holistic view of the place of human beings in the world. I hope that feminists will bear this in mind when they see the word 'man' used in this book and take it as a compliment and not a slight. But it will, I fear, take more than feminism to shift us from our anthropocentric view of the world and see ourselves, as God sees us, as part of a wonderful and complex chain of being, each part of which is as precious and vital as the next.

The best place to find out how God views us, and indeed to begin our escape from anthropocentrism, is in those majestic opening chapters of Genesis which unfold the great Judaeo–Christian myth of creation. I use the word myth advisedly, not to imply that the Genesis story is untrue but to suggest that the truth which it contains is not of a literal or factual kind. Outside the creationist movement there are surely few

Christian believers now who take the biblical account of creation as a piece of factual history which describes how the world came into being. Its truth lies rather in what it tells us about God's relationship with this world and his method of operating within it. This way of looking at the creation story rescues it from the realm of remote primeval history and gives it a greater relevance to us now. It is to be read as a deeply considered piece of poetic and spiritual writing rather than as a scientific account of how the world began.

There are two biblical accounts of creation – one in the first chapter of Genesis and another in the second. They contrast markedly in both form and content and convey very different messages about the relationship between humans and the rest of creation. Confusingly the second account, which is from the J or Yahwehist source (so called because it uses the Hebrew term *Yahweh* for God), is the older, dating from around 950 BC. The story which appears in the first chapter comes from the so-called Priestly document which was composed four or five hundred years later.

There is no mention of man's dominion over the rest of creation in the Yahwehist story. The image which it projects of human relations with nature is one of companionship and stewardship. The animal kingdom is brought into being so that humans are not alone and Adam is put into the Garden of Eden 'to till it and keep it' (Gen. 2:15). But we can hardly ignore the commission to man to exercise dominion over the rest of the earth that occurs in the later Priestly account. It is found not only in Genesis 1:26 but is repeated and strengthened in 1:28 where man is told to 'fill the earth and subdue it'. Almost exactly the same words crop up again in Psalm 8 in a meditation on the human condition which begins 'what is man that thou are mindful of him' (8:4) and concludes with the answer:

Yet thou hast made him little less than God,
   and dost crown him with glory and honour.
Thou has given him dominion over the works of thy hands;
   thou hast put all things under his feet,
all sheep and oxen,

and also the beasts of the field,
the birds of the air, and the fish of the sea,
    whatever passes along the paths of the sea. (Ps. 8:5–8)

On the face of it these verses do seem to give man carte
blanche to do what he will with the rest of creation. Three
different Hebrew verbs are used in them to describe the
relationship between humans and others. All have a strong
sense of power and are associated with the rule of kings. In
other parts of the Old Testament they are variously translated
as tread down, dominate, rule, bring into bondage, oppress,
beat, assault and force.

If, however, we look more closely at the overall context in
which these words occur in Genesis 1 we get a rather different
picture of what is meant by dominion in this particular
instance. Even a cursory reading of the Priestly story reveals
certain things which at least throw a question mark over the
traditional interpretation of its closing verses. Taken as a
whole it is quite clear that the dominant theme is not man's
dominion over nature but God's total lordship over the entire
cosmos. The whole thrust of the narrative is to assert that
God alone is in charge – it is his unaided creative power that
subdues the forces of chaos and sustains the world in being
and everything that exists belongs to him. He alone can be
described as lord of creation. He has, in the words of a
popular chorus, got the whole world in his hands, or as the
psalmist more majestically puts it, 'The earth is the Lord's
and the fullness thereof' (Ps. 24:1).

It is also abundantly clear from the Priestly account of
creation that man is not the only object of God's interest and
concern. Its subject is the creation of the world as a whole
and not just of man. At every stage of the story that unfolds
we are told emphatically that God saw what he had made
and found it to be good. In other words he found goodness
in many things apart from his creation of human beings. Men
and women come last upon the scene and they may be pictured to some extent as the crowning glory of creation but
they are not portrayed as having the right to do as they wish
with everything else that was created before them. Rather

16

they stand before God as creatures just as dependent on him for their life and breath and their very being as the simplest amoeba.

It is true that in one key respect humans are portrayed as being unique. Genesis 1:27 tells us that they are created in the image of God, something which does not seem to apply to any other creatures. Much effort has been expended in trying to establish what this phrase means and specifically to work out in what ways human beings do resemble God. Is it in possessing reason or in having an immortal soul? In fact modern Old Testament scholarship suggests that the Hebrew word traditionally translated as image might rather more faithfully be rendered as representative and conveys the idea of man as God's agent on earth. Such an interpretation opens the way to seeing humans as stewards of creation rather than its lords. But even if we keep to the traditional idea of the *imago Dei* and see man as made uniquely in the likeness of God we arrive at a similar idea of his position *vis-à-vis* the rest of creation. In so far as we can fathom what must always remain a great and holy mystery, chief among the characteristics of the God Christians worship must surely come creativity, justice and an overwhelming and overflowing love which knows no bounds. The days are thankfully largely gone when the Almighty was seen in the guise of a celestial Roman emperor or medieval monarch and characterised by such attributes as omnipotence, wrath and domination. If human beings are uniquely created in God's image then that surely means that they are made to exercise the virtues which particularly distinguish him. That is hardly compatible with a commission to exploit the rest of creation.

If the phrase 'image of God' may have been misunderstood over the Christian centuries, this has been even more true of the key word 'dominion' which is used in Genesis 1 to describe the proper relationship between humans and the rest of creation. We have already noted that the original Hebrew words were associated with the rule of kings. In the ancient Israelite world monarchs were not seen as absolutist and despotic figures but as the viceregents and deputies of God on earth, holding their power on trust from him and charged with exercising mercy and justice towards his creatures. It is this kind of rule that the Priestly author had in mind when he recorded God's commission to humans to have dominion over the earth. It is not a matter of someone handing over power to another but of the Lord of all things giving a solemn trust and responsibility to one of his creatures for the welfare and order of the rest.

In his monumental commentary on the opening chapters of Genesis, Claus Westermann categorically refutes the idea that the dominion given by God to humans over the animal world should be interpreted as a mandate for exploitation. He points to the importance in Hebrew thought of the category of living things, or *nefesh hayya*, in which humans are bound together with beasts, birds, fishes and insects. He also points out that dominion certainly does not include the right to kill animals for food since the Priestly creation story (and also the Yahwehist account in Genesis 2) portrays humans as vegetarians with the fruits of plants and trees for their food. 'People would forfeit their kingly role among the living,' he writes, 'were the animals to be made the object of their whim.'[8] In Westermann's view the words generally translated as dominion in the creation story are there to suggest a primacy for humans in the hierarchy of the animal kingdom. In a way they are perhaps to be read as an acknowledgement of the evolutionary principle and of the fact that *Homo sapiens* is the most highly developed species yet to appear on earth. They provide a way of classifying and ordering the world of living things. Interestingly the same words are used to describe the sun's relationship with the moon and the stars, establishing a similar hierarchy in the world of planets. If there is a more direct message in God's commission to humans in Genesis 1:26, 28, it is to stress that they should have a personal relationship with living creatures just as a good ruler should have a personal relationship with his people.

The Old Testament as a whole stresses the oneness of human beings and other living creatures that derives from their membership of the category of *nefesh hayya*. But it also sees a more fundamental link binding man with the rest of creation. There is no word in ancient Hebrew corresponding to our word 'nature' and that is simply because the ancient Israelites had no concept of a separate world of nature existing over and against the world of human beings. As we have already seen, the whole stress in Old Testament theology is on God as the Lord of all creation. This leads to a profoundly holistic world picture in which humans take their place with every other creature in a state of utter dependence on God. There is a strong sense too of the interdependence of all creatures and an image of the world as a single cosmic community rather than a collection of autonomous entities.

It is interesting that modern science is increasingly conceiving of the world in very similar terms as a unified and interdependent community. Quantum physics suggests that at the deepest level the universe is a single unified whole, indivisible and bound together by a simple yet powerful force. Biologists talk in similar language, expressed most dramatically, perhaps, in Professor James Lovelock's Gaia hypothesis which states that 'the entire range of living matter on Earth, from whales to viruses and from oaks to algae, could be regarded as constituting a single living entity'.[9] This way of describing the world in which we live would have struck a deep chord with the writers of the Old Testament. Several thousand years before the discovery of the unified gravitational force or the DNA molecule they had grasped the essential unity of the cosmos, a unity which they saw as deriving from the radical dependence of every part of creation on the one true and living God.

This sense of the oneness between humans and the rest of creation is an important corrective both to the idea that man has been put into the world to dominate nature and also to the notion that somehow raw nature is superior to man and could get along better without him. It is powerfully expressed in the Hebrew word for man, *Adam*, which is derived from the word for earth, *Adama*. In the Yahwehist account of creation in Genesis 2 this link is given particular force when God is portrayed as creating man out of the dust of the ground. Later in the story of the fall, God tells Adam that he will return to the ground out of which he was taken, since 'you are dust, and to dust you shall return' (Gen. 3:19). This same message of the essential unity between humans, animals and the inanimate elements of creation is beautifully conveyed in Eliphaz the Temanite's assurance to the prophet Job that if he follows God he will be at one with the physical and animal world, 'For you shall be in the league with the stones of the field, and the beasts of the field shall be at peace with you' (Job 5:23).

The unity between humans and all other living creatures is also a central theme in the biblical story of the flood. At one level this can, of course, be read as a powerful reminder of the point established in the creation narratives that God alone is the lord of all with the power to destroy as well as to create life. It also reflects an awareness of the ambiguity of nature and of the ever-present forces of chaos which have been reined in by God but not completely banished from the cosmos. The implications of both these points will be explored in later chapters. But the tale of Noah and his ark is also an ecological parable which tells of God's concern for all his creatures and points to the role of humans as stewards and protectors of other species. The commission which the Lord addresses to Noah before the flood is very different from that given in Genesis 1:26:

> For behold, I will bring a flood of waters upon the earth, to destroy all flesh in which is the breath of life under heaven; everything that is on the earth shall die. But I will establish my covenant with you; and you shall come into the ark, you, your sons, your wife, and your sons' wives with you. And of every living thing of all flesh, you shall bring two of every sort into the ark, to keep them alive with you; they shall be male and female. Of the birds according to their kinds, and of the animals according to their kinds, and of every creeping thing of the ground according to its kind, two of every sort shall come in with you, to keep them alive. (Gen. 6:17–20)

Cramped together in the ark, tossed by the waves and at last beached on Mount Ararat, animals and humans share a common life and a common destiny. It is indeed a microcosm of our existence on the planet earth – crowded, precarious, bound together in the struggle for survival, dependent on each other and above all on him who never completely abandons us. When the water at last subsides and chaos gives way to calm, the everlasting covenant which God makes is not just with Noah:

> Behold, I establish my covenant with you and your descendants after you, and with every living creature that is with you, the birds, the cattle, and every beast of the earth with you, as many as came out of the ark. I establish my covenant with you that never again shall all flesh be cut off by the waters of a flood, and never again shall there be a flood to destroy the earth. (Gen. 9:9–11).

The theme that comes across in this passage of God's concern for all of his creation is developed much more explicitly in the Psalms. In those great hymns of praise Yahweh is worshipped not only as the Lord of history who has brought the Israelites out of slavery but also as the Lord of creation who sustains in being all that is and for whom every part of creation has a significance and purpose in its own right and not just for its usefulness to man:

> The trees of the Lord are watered abundantly,
>   the cedars of Lebanon which he planted.
> In them the birds build their nests;
>   the stork has her home in the fir trees.
> The high mountains are for the wild goats;
>   the rocks are a refuge for the badgers.
> Thou hast made the moon to mark the seasons;
>   the sun knows its time for setting.
> Thou makest darkness, and it is night,
>   when all the beasts of the forest creep forth.
> The young lions roar for their prey,
>   seeking their food from God.
> When the sun rises, they get them away
>   and lie down in their dens.

Man goes forth to his work
and to his labour until the evening. (Ps. 104:16–23)

What is striking about that passage is the way man is
thrown in almost as an afterthought and an aside. As the
contemporary Anglican theologian John Austin Baker puts
it, the psalmist 'places him, with great artistry, in the context
of all the other teeming life of the earth. Nothing is done to
highlight him; he is just another figure in the landscape'.[10]
The emphasis is very different from that suggested in the
opening chapter of Genesis, at least as it has been convention-
ally interpreted, and misinterpreted, from our anthropocentric perspective. In the Psalms, and in the latter part of
the Old Testament as a whole, all creatures are placed on an
equal footing in the wonderful order of God's world and
human beings are generally not singled out for special treatment. At times indeed humans are radically cut down to size
and reminded that they are just as frail and transitory as the
rest of God's creation:

As for man, his days are as grass: as a flower of the field,
so he flourisheth. For the wind passeth over it, and it is
gone; and the place thereof shall know it no more. (Ps.
103:15–16 AV)

What does man gain by all the toil
at which he toils under the sun?
A generation goes, and a generation comes,
but the earth remains for ever. (Eccles. 1:3–4)

For the fate of the sons of men and the fate of beasts is the
same; as one dies, so dies the other. They all have the same
breath, and man has no advantage over the beasts. (Eccles.
3:19)

Nowhere in the Bible is our besetting sin of anthropocentrism tackled more directly and effectively than in the Book of
Job. It is there that we get the sharpest reminder that the
universe does not revolve around us. Again and again Job

cries to God for an explanation of his suffering, voicing that
most persistent and perplexing question about human existence – why is there so much misery and pain in our lives?
The response comes not in the form of an answer but in a
series of questions that God puts to the prophet:

Where were you when I laid the foundation of the earth?
    Tell me, if you have understanding.
Who determined its measurement – surely you know!
    Or who stretched the line upon it?
On what were its bases sunk,
    or who laid the cornerstone,
when the morning stars sang together,
    and all the sons of God shouted for joy? (Job 38:4–7)

Have you entered into the springs of the sea,
    or walked in the recesses of the deep?
Have the gates of death been revealed to you,
    or have you seen the gates of deep darkness?
Have you comprehended the expanse of the earth?
    Declare, if you know all this. (Job 38:16–18)

Who has cleft a channel for the torrents of rain,
    and a way for the thunderbolt,
to bring rain on a land where no man is,
    on the desert in which there is no man;
to satisfy the waste and desolate land,
    and to make the ground put forth grass? (Job 38:25–27)

Can you lift up your voice to the clouds,
    that a flood of waters may cover you?
Can you send forth lightnings, that they may go
    and say to you, 'Here we are'?
Who has put wisdom in the clouds,
    or given understanding to the mists? (Job 38:34–36)

Who has let the wild ass go free?
    Who has loosed the bonds of the swift ass,
to whom I have given the steppe for his home,
    and the salt land for his dwelling place?
He scorns the tumult of the city;

he hears not the shouts of the driver.
He ranges the mountains as his pasture,
   and he searches after every green thing. (Job 39:5–8)

There are two rather different answers to Job's question that one might draw from these remarkable passages. One is that humans are pretty insignificant in the whole order of God's creation and that they do not really have much use or purpose in his divine plan. Christians have sometimes been tempted to such a view. There is a touching poem by George Herbert called 'Employment' which pictures man as rather useless compared with much in the world of nature:

> If as a flower doth spread and die,
> Thou wouldst extend me to some good,
> Before I were by frost's extremity
>   Nipt in the bud;
>
> All things are busy: only I
> Neither bring honey with the bees
> Nor flowers to make that, nor the husbandry
>   To water these.
>
> I am no link of thy great chain
> But all my company is a weed.
> Lord, place me in thy consort; give one strain
>   To my poor reed.

But this is not exactly the message that the author of the Book of Job is trying to convey. The other answer is that he is seeking to dispel the idea that everything revolves round man by stressing the value to God in their own right of the other parts of creation rather than by suggesting that humans are of no importance. John Baker has commented of God's speech to Job that

> the wonders of the natural order are used for a didactic purpose unique in the Bible, and possibly in all ancient literature: namely, to make the point that man's whole attitude to what goes on in the created order is wrong,

because it is totally egoistic, totally anthropocentric. If he were to stop for even a moment to consider the universe as it actually is, he would see that by far the greatest part of it has no relevance to him at all.[11]

It is not so much that man is diminished but that the value of the animals, the birds, the plants and the inanimate elements of earth and water is stressed in their own right. They do not exist just for man's use and enjoyment. As Thomas Gray put it in his *Elegy written in a Country Churchyard*:

> Full many a gem of purest ray serene
> The dark unfathom'd caves of ocean bear:
> Full many a flower is born to blush unseen,
> And waste its sweetness on the desert air.

The questions that God puts to Job go to the heart of our present ecological crisis. They make clear his concern for every threatened species of plant and animal, with every part of his creation which is destroyed by humans because it seems to them to be useless or expendable. It is perhaps significant that in his final speech to the perplexed prophet the Lord points to the beauty and primacy of the great sea monster Leviathan, the ancestor and prototype of the whales we are now hunting to extinction:

> Can you fill his skin with harpoons,
>   or his head with fishing spears?
> Lay hand on him;
>   think of the battle; you will not do it again!
> (Job 41:7–8)

Sea monsters occupy a remarkable place in the Old Testament. They are the first specific creatures to be mentioned in the creation account in Genesis 1; Psalm 104 proclaims that Leviathan was made by God to sport in the sea; and in Psalm 148 sea monsters head the list of the creatures giving praise to God. In the Book of Jonah it is of course a whale that is made the instrument of the prophet's salvation and repentance. Jonah's sojourn of three days and nights in the belly of the whale is picked up by Jesus in Matthew 12:39 as a symbol of his own death, burial and resurrection. In both Celtic and medieval Christianity whales had a special significance. As he stood on the shore of Iona St Columba often prayed that he might see a sea monster, the greatest of all God's creatures. During their stormy voyage from Ireland to the northern and western islands off Scotland St Brendan and his followers spent their Easter vigil on what they took at first to be an island but which later proved to be a whale. As a result whales came to be associated in Ireland with Easter. In a recent article deploring the virtual extinction of ten whale species the theologian and ecologist Edward Echlin writes:

> Solidarity with the whale has been within the Christian tradition as long as there have been Christians . . . God's people will not take kindly to the extinction of Leviathan. He's been part of their warp and woof for too long a time, ever since their Master uttered those unforgettable words about the sign of Jonah.[12]

Saving the whale is not the only contemporary Green crusade which receives powerful endorsement from the Scriptures. So also does the whole campaign to move away from intensive high-input farming towards organic husbandry. It is hardly surprising that the Old Testament should contain a good deal of advice on the subject of good agricultural practice. It is, after all, the story of the settlement of a nomadic people, the Israelites, in a fertile land where they can grow crops and keep animals. There is much in the earlier books of the Bible in particular on the attitude that should be adopted to both the treatment and the ownership of land in the light of the guiding belief that the earth belongs to the Lord. Some of it may seem archaic today but if we are to live by that same conviction and, indeed, to save our earth from pollution and destruction we would do well to heed the words of the Old Testament prophets and law-givers.

The respect with which the ancient Israelites treated the earth was a reflection not just of their sense that it belonged to God but also of their experience in coming from a land of desert and wilderness. They knew only too well how precious springs of water and fertile soil were and how they needed to be conserved and respected. Again and again God is praised by the psalmists and prophets as the one who has led his people through the desert and the parched and thirsty ground to the 'land of hills and valleys, which drinks water by the rain of heaven'. The Lord is worshipped as the bringer of rain just as much as the one who has saved his people. It is significant how many of the great encounters recorded between humans and God, or his messengers, in both the Old and New Testaments take place near wells or springs. Water was a sacred and precious possession, a gift from God not to be treated lightly or wasted.

This same feeling extended to the land itself. The Israelites were only too aware of how precarious was the dividing line between fertile soil and barren desert. Few were more conscious of this than the prophet Jeremiah who lived in the village of Anatot on the edge of the Judaean desert. From his house he looked west to the lush greenery of the Judaean hills covered in vineyards and fields of grain. If he looked the other way he saw only bare rock and sand. Jeremiah was terrified that through the greed and rapacity of man the fertile land would be destroyed and the desert spread westwards:

> Many shepherds have destroyed my vineyard,
>   they have trampled down my portion,
> they have made my pleasant portion
>   a desolate wilderness;
> They have made it a desolation;
>   desolate, it mourns to me.
> The whole land is made desolate,
>   but no man lays it to heart. (Jer. 12:10–11)

Today we are equally conscious of the extent to which over-intensive agriculture can lead to dust bowls and 'desertification' but this does not stop us continuing with methods of irrigation and cultivation which remove the topsoil from large areas of land. We also continue to exhaust the soil with a non-stop cycle of sowing and cropping, pausing only to poison it with massive doses of chemical fertilisers and pesticides. The result has been not only over-production of cereals and other agricultural products but a serious depletion in the quantity and quality of the humus. EEC governments have recently started paying farmers to set aside part of their land from cultivation. Three thousand years ago the Israelites knew the importance of regularly letting the land lie fallow and not practising intensive husbandry. For them the idea of the Sabbath as a time of rest did not apply just to human beings. The laws that God gave to Moses on Mount Sinai following the Ten Commandments make clear that it was equally applicable to the ox and the ass (Exod. 23:12) and indeed to the land itself:

> The Lord said to Moses on Mount Sinai, 'Say to the people of Israel, When you come into the land which I give you, the land shall keep a sabbath to the Lord. Six years you shall sow your field, and six years you shall prune your vineyard, and gather in its fruits; but in the seventh year there shall be a sabbath of solemn rest for the land, a sabbath to the Lord; you shall not sow your field or prune your vineyard. What grows of itself in your harvest you shall not reap, and the grapes of your undressed vine you shall not gather; it shall be a year of solemn rest for the land. (Lev. 25:1–5).

If the principle that the earth belongs to the Lord produced a clearly ecological attitude towards the treatment of the earth in the Old Testament then it also led to a radical approach towards land ownership. The Hebrew land laws, which occupy much space in the early books of the Bible, were based on the simple premiss that God is the only landlord and that he alone has an absolute right to own property. As far as human beings are concerned entitlement to land is always spoken of in terms of possession or inheritance and never in terms of ownership or property. When they reached the Promised Land the families of the tribes of Israel were allocated plots of ground on a strict principle of equality. They held these plots as trustees for their descendants and were specifically forbidden to buy or sell them. 'The land shall not be sold in perpetuity', the Lord told Moses on Mount Sinai, 'for the land is mine; for you are strangers and sojourners with me' (Lev. 25:23).

The Hebrew land laws did allow the leasing of land but only for a limited period. Every fifty years there was a year of Jubilee when all leases fell in, all outstanding debts were cancelled and all plots of land reverted to the descendants of those who had originally been granted them. How far these laws were enforced is unclear: certainly the eighth-century prophets railed against their contemporaries for accumulating land whether by purchase or by more devious means:

Woe to those who join house to house,
    who add field to field,
until there is no more room,
    and you are made to dwell alone
    in the midst of the land. (Isa. 5:8)

Wicked men move boundary-stones
and carry away flocks and their shepherds.
In the field they reap what is not theirs,
and filch the late grapes from the rich man's vineyard.
They drive off the orphan's ass
and lead away the widow's ox with a rope.
                                (Job. 24:2–3 NEB)

Woe to those who devise wickedness . . .
    They covet fields and seize them. (Micah 2:1–2)

The idea that private ownership and exploitation of the land is contrary to God's law is continued in the New Testament and the life of the early Church. Jesus announced that he had come to proclaim the year of Jubilee, and his followers in the early Church practised a form of agrarian communism: 'they had everything in common . . . as many as were possessors of lands or houses sold them, and brought the proceeds of what was sold and laid it at the apostles' feet; and distribution was made to each as any had need' (Acts 4:32, 34–35).

At the end of the sixth century Pope Gregory the Great
made a strong attack on those who regarded land as private
property to be bought and sold rather than as a gift of God,
describing them as the murderers of the poor. Five hundred
years later Hildegarde of Bingen picked up that other strongly
ecological theme in the Old Testament approach to land
when she stressed the fertility and goodness of the earth
and the importance of treating it with respect. In the mid-
seventeenth century the English religious and social radical
Gerrard Winstanley, leader of the Digger movement, argued
that man's original sin lay in exploiting and acquiring private
ownership over what God had intended to be the common
treasury of the land.

Similarly radical statements about the land based soundly
on biblical teaching have continued to be made by Christian
people faced with oppression and injustice in more recent
times. When at the end of the nineteenth century the crofters
of the Scottish highlands and islands finally fought back
against the lairds who had cleared them off the land to make
room for more profitable sheep and deer parks they rallied
behind banners declaring 'The earth is the Lord's and the
fullness thereof'. Among the most impressive practical results
of the spread of liberation theology in Latin America has
been a movement to restore land to the peasants. A document
published by the Brazilian bishops in 1986 entitled 'Liberate
the Land' quoted the Jubilee laws of Deuteronomy and Leviti-
cus in support of its argument that the concentration of land
in the hands of a few wealthy people is sinful and contrary
to the Gospel.

All this takes us a long way from the understanding of
human dominion over nature that has traditionally been
derived from the Bible, and from the opening chapters of
Genesis in particular. The fact is that the Old Testament
gives no warrant at all for exploitative and instrumental attitudes on the part of human beings towards the rest of creation.
Quite the reverse. But if this is indeed the case we are entitled
to ask why such attitudes have entered so very firmly into
the Christian tradition, for that they are there is undeniable.
The answer is that they have come in via those various alien

philosophies and heresies which have been caught up and enmeshed in Christianity over the ages. As we have seen, the idea of a radical separation between human beings and the world of nature was totally foreign to Hebrew thought but it is deeply embedded in ancient Greek philosophy. The Stoics in particular preached the superiority of man over nature. The effect of this alien Hellenistic strand in early Christianity was greatly compounded by the influence of the Gnostics with their dualistic teaching on the gulf that separated the physical and spiritual worlds and their insistence that all matter was corrupt and sinful. In more recent times it has been confirmed by the dominance of Cartesian dualism between mind and matter in western philosophy and by the rise of a scientific outlook which has seen the natural world as an object to be quantified, measured and then used for man's good rather than as an integral part of God's creation to be approached with wonder, love and praise. All these forces have contributed to an outlook which regards human beings as having a totally different destiny from the rest of creation.

This way of looking at the world may at last be changing. In the latter part of the twentieth century science has taken a new turn which makes it much more sympathetic to a holistic view of the relationship between humans and nature. Until comparatively recently physics asserted that the knowing scientist could be detached and separated from what he or she was describing. It dealt with a world that was not altered by the scientist's act of knowing. Now the theories of relativity and quantum physics have shown that observer and observed cannot be separated in this way, that indeed the very act of describing nature involves a partial determination of its properties. In the words of Richard Schlegel, 'man has been returned into physics, after an absence of several hundred years'.[13] It may well be that it will be scientists who break down the distinctions between the human and the natural spheres that have bedevilled western thought for so long.

There have, thank God, always been some Christians prepared to resist the relentless tide of anthropocentrism and hold fast to the biblical doctrine that the earth is the Lord's and the fullness thereof. They have stressed the plenitude and variety of God's works, the fecundity of the Creator and the fact that everything that exists has a value and worth in his sight – from the great cedars of Lebanon and the mighty sea monster Leviathan to the lilies of the field and the sparrow falling from heaven. Thomas Aquinas expressed this sensitively in his *Summa Theologiae*:

> God brought things into being in order that His goodness might be communicated to creatures and represented by them; and because His goodness could not be adequately represented by one creature alone. He produced many and diverse creatures so that what was wanting to one in the manifestation of the divine goodness might be supplied by another. For goodness which in God is simple and uniform, in creatures is manifold and divided; and hence the whole universe together participates in the divine goodness more perfectly and represents it better than any single creature whatever.[14]

Once we really grasp this idea of the pleroma or fullness of God's creation and the significance of every part of it to him then we can surely no longer go on destroying the whales, cutting down the tropical rain forests or turning the good earth into dust bowls and deserts. If we go back to the very end of the first account of creation in Genesis we find it clearly spelt out that 'God saw everything that he had made, and behold it was very good'. If we pondered the meaning of that verse rather more and spent a little less time on the one that comes just a little earlier, our views on the proper relationship between humans and the rest of creation might be rather different. In the words of Claus Westermann:

> The simple fact that the first page of the Bible speaks about heaven and earth, the sun, moon and stars, about plants and trees, about birds, fish and animals, is a certain sign that the God whom we acknowledge in the Creed as the Father of Jesus Christ is concerned with all of these creatures, and not merely with humans. A God who is understood only as the god of humankind is no longer the God of the Bible.[15]

2

The dance of creation
The trees of the field shall clap their hands

The doctrine of human dominion over the rest of creation is not the only recipe for environmental disaster which Christianity has been blamed for producing. Equally damaging in the eyes of many Greens is the notion that the world of nature is wholly profane, without any sacred or mysterious quality and therefore fair game to be objectified and exploited. Once again we can turn to Lynn White's seminal article on 'the historical roots of our ecologic crisis' for a trenchant exposition of this particular charge against Christianity:

> In Antiquity every tree, every spring, every stream, every hill had its own genius loci, its guardian spirit . . . Before one cut a tree, mined a mountain, or damned a brook, it was important to placate the spirit in charge of that particular situation, and to keep it placated. By destroying pagan animism, Christianity made it possible to exploit nature in a mood of indifference to the feelings of natural objects . . . The spirits in natural objects, which formerly had protected nature from man, evaporated. Man's effective monopoly on spirit in this world was confirmed, and the old inhibitions to the exploitation of nature crumbled.[1]

Strictly, of course, it is the Hebrew religion rather than Christianity that should bear the brunt of this charge. Its radical monotheism swept away the great multiplicity of divinities worshipped in pagan religions and located in rivers, trees and mountains. But it is true that Christianity largely took over this aspect of the ancient Jewish faith as it took over so many others. The result, so the argument goes, has been to rob nature of all its mystery and sanctity and render it at best simply neutral and at worst wholly profane.

One possible, though much debated, consequence of this has been the rise of science in the West. It is often argued that by demythologising and desacralising the natural world Christianity opened the way for it to be observed, analysed and measured. Nature became an object of intellectual interest rather than worship. There is now some doubt about this – indeed there is a counter-agreement, which will be considered in Chapter 3, that the advance of science was actually delayed in the western world because of the power of the Christian idea of nature as corrupt and fallen. But it is certainly tempting to see the flourishing of science and technology in the Christianised western hemisphere as somehow linked to the prevalent view of nature as a neutral and objective sphere which contrasts strongly with the animism and nature-worship of most eastern religions. God was not left out of the picture altogether but he tended to be cast in the role of the Divine watchmaker who had made a perfectly designed world and then sat back while it ticked away. Indeed the intricate design and intelligibility of the world became an important argument in natural theology and a key proof of God's existence. The reasoning went that if the world was indeed intelligible to man and capable of scientific study and measurement then it must have been created by a supremely intelligent and rational being and not just the product of chance. But until very recent times scientists and the wider public have had little sense of God being actively involved in his creation. They might marvel at the intricacy and order of nature but they have approached it in a spirit of detached objectivity and not in a spirit of awe and wonder. It has been seen as a laboratory rather than a mystery.

There is no doubt that this view of nature has characterised much Christian thought over the last 1500 years. St Augustine must take much of the blame for giving western Christianity its dualistic sense of the world being divided into matter and spirit, with the one basically corrupt and the other good. Despite his attempts to shake off his Manichean past, he was never able to rid himself of a sense of revulsion against all things physical, including the human body. The Protestant Reformers were also deeply suspicious of the natural world, doing their best to stamp out what they took to be the last vestiges of pagan animism in the Catholic practices of associating saints with wells and springs. By seeing God as Lord of history rather than Lord of creation and concentrating almost entirely on the theme of human salvation, they relegated nature to at best a backdrop against which the great drama of God's interaction with his human creatures was played out. This picture has continued to dominate both Protestant and Roman Catholic theology until comparatively recently. As recently as 1963 a liberal Anglican commenting on the interpretation of the miracles could write that 'Nature merely furnishes the stage for the major work of God. This takes place in the realm of history.'[2]

This reductionist and disparaging view of the material world in general, and the realm of nature in particular, is wholly at odds with the message of the Bible. We have already seen that Genesis portrays God as saying that everything he has made is good and that the Old Testament as a whole clearly and constantly affirms his interest and involvement in the totality of his creation. The New Testament takes this involvement a stage further by introducing the whole idea of the Incarnation. Far from shunning the physical and material and seeing it as profane or corrupt, God clothes himself in the form of a human body and sends his Son to tread this earth. As is made so clear in the epistles of St Paul, so often and so wrongly thought to perpetrate a kind of dualism and to be hostile to the world of matter, the whole emphasis in Christian eschatology and hope about the life to come is on the resurrection of the body rather than on the Hellenistic idea of the immortality of the soul. Christian worship is based on the administration of sacraments which testify to the deep sacredness of the physical elements of water, wine and bread. William Temple has rightly described Christianity as 'the most materialistic of all great religions. The others hope to achieve spiritual reality by ignoring matter – calling it illusion or saying that it does not exist . . . Christianity, based as it is on the Incarnation, regards matter as destined to be the vehicle and instrument of spirit.'[3]

So how did these alien ideas of physical matter as corrupt and nature as profane become so firmly rooted in the Christian tradition? The explanation lies in the pervasive power of our two old friends, human anthropocentrism and the dualistic philosophy of the Greeks and the Gnostics. By putting humans at the centre of everything we have relegated nature to the periphery. We have pictured God in our own image as the Lord of history rather than the Lord of creation. We have seen his mighty acts only in such human dramas as the exodus of the Israelites from Egypt to the Promised Land and not in the tremendous physical energy and activity that characterises the universe. We have largely assimilated the view of the ancient Greeks that all physical matter is corrupt because it is subject to decay and that only the purely spiritual is good. We have also been influenced much more that we would care to admit by Gnosticism, Manicheanism and other similar heresies which have refused to accept the orthodox Christian doctrine that God created everything out of nothing and have seen rather a dualistic world of evil matter and good spirit existing from the beginning. Somehow we have also managed to convince ourselves that in this world humans are firmly on the spiritual rather than the physical side. This has involved a quite un-Christian denial of the sanctity of the body, wholly at odds with St Paul's description of it as the temple of the spirit. It has also led us to regard God as only having a relationship with the human element in his creation, and only with a rather limited part of it at that. It is only through our minds and souls that we seem to feel we can communicate with God – our bodies we tend to consign along with the rest of nature to the realm of the profane.

The implications of this kind of thinking are extraordinary. Are we really saying that God had nothing to do with the world for the billions of years until *Homo sapiens* came on the scene? Is the One who created the entire cosmos and found everything in it good only interested in just one of the millions of species he has created? Our conceit is incredible and is also quite unfounded. The Bible clearly proclaims God to be

Lord of the cosmos as well as Lord of history, involved in an active relationship with the whole of his creation and not just with the human part.

It is true that the Old Testament points to a single God who is transcendent and separate from the world which he has created. The ancient Israelites were keen to distance themselves from the pagan cults which had a multiplicity of divinities and which worshipped nature *per se*. In its transcendent monotheism, indeed Hebrew religion provides a useful buttress against the temptation which is perhaps gaining ground in some quarters of the Green movement to hark back to pagan animism, worshipping raw nature and seeing man as a largely destructive and unwelcome intrusion. But it is entirely wrong to see the God of the Old Testament as simply being interested in humans and not interacting with nature. It is also wrong to see the natural world being portrayed as profane and without any capacity to respond to God.

Yehuda Feliks, a modern Jewish scholar of the Hebrew Scriptures, has written a beautifully illustrated study of *Nature and Man in the Bible*, published in 1981. He argues with considerable supporting textual evidence that the Bible is first and foremost a book about nature and only secondly a book about man:

> A comparison of the descriptions of nature in the Bible with those in the literature of the ancient East and in the ancient Greek epics shows that in the Bible are to be found pictures of nature which in strength of expression are unparalleled in any of the other ancient literary creations.[4]

He finds the whole of the Old Testament to be deeply imbued with a consciousness of Divine Providence over the whole of creation 'from the cedar tree that is in Lebanon even unto the hyssop that springeth out of the wall' (1 Kgs 4:33 AV).

There is certainly a clear impression conveyed throughout the Old Testament that God enjoys a personal relationship with the world of nature. We encounter it first near the beginning of the creation account in the first chapter of Genesis when, in response to God's command, the elements of light and darkness, earth and heaven spring into being. In the words of George Hendry, 'As God said to Abraham, "Go from your country," and Abraham went "as the Lord had told him" (Genesis 12:1–4), so he said, "Let there be light," and there was light (Genesis 1:3). In both realms He acts by word and in both his word is obeyed.'⁵ This theme of God addressing the elements recurs again and again:

> For to the snow he says, 'Fall on the earth',
> And to the shower and the rain, 'Be strong'. (Job. 37:6)

> The waters stood above the mountains.
> At thy rebuke they fled. (Ps. 104:6–7)

The impression here is that the inert physical elements of creation know just as well as human beings who is in charge. George Herbert picked up the point in his poem 'The Church Militant':

> Almighty Lord, who from thy glorious throne
> Seest and rulest all things ev'n as one:
> The smallest ant or atom knows thy power,
> Known also to each minute of an hour.

A somewhat different theme which is pursued in particular by the prophets is that of God using animals against human beings because of their pride and sinfulness. Sometimes they are portrayed simply as agents of divine punishment. Jeremiah reflects on what will happen to those of his countrymen who have broken the laws of God:

> . . . A lion from the forest shall slay them,
> a wolf from the desert shall destroy them.
> A leopard is watching against their cities,
> every one who goes out of them shall be torn to pieces.
> (Jer. 5:6)

> I will appoint over them four kinds of destroyers, says the Lord: the sword to slay, the dogs to tear, and the birds of

the air and the beasts of the earth to devour and destroy.
(Jer. 15:3)

Animals and birds are also used in a rather gentler way to
upbraid human beings, their faithfulness and steadfastness
being compared favourably to the waywardness of man:

> Even the stork in the heavens
>   knows her times;
> and the turtledove, swallow, and crane
>   keep the time of their coming;
> but my people know not
>   the ordinance of the Lord. (Jer. 8:7)

If this was the only kind of reference that we found in the
Old Testament to God's dealings with his non-human creation then we might be justified in viewing nature in purely
instrumental terms, as an object which God orders around
and an agent which he uses for the punishment and instruc-
tion of humans. But the relationship which the Bible describes
between God and nature is very much more positive and
dynamic than this. It is a dialogue in which the natural world
is pictured as responding to the lure and love of its Creator.
Just as women and men can reach up to God in prayer and
adoration, so also the birds and animals can lift their voices
to him in song, the rivers and streams can gurgle their joy,
the trees of the field can clap their hands, the mountains and
the hills can skip forth like goats. It is almost as though every
created being is an instrument in a cosmic orchestra, giving
its own distinctive tune to the great symphony that is being
played in response to the biddings of the unseen conductor.

The Psalms in particular contain some beautiful evocations
of the entire created order praising God:

> Praise the Lord!
> Praise the Lord from the heavens,
>   praise him in the heights!
> Praise him, all his angels,
>   praise him, all his host!

Praise him, sun and moon,
   praise him, all you shining stars!
Praise him, you highest heavens,
   and you waters above the heavens!

Praise the Lord from the earth,
   you sea monsters and all deeps,
fire and hail, snow and frost,
   stormy wind fulfilling his command!
Mountains and all hills,
   fruit trees and all cedars!
Beasts and all cattle,
   creeping things and flying birds! (Ps. 148:1–4, 7–10)

Let the heavens be glad, and let the earth rejoice;
   let the sea roar, and all that fills it;
   let the field exult, and everything in it!
Then shall all the trees of the wood sing for joy
   before the Lord. (Ps. 96:11–13)

Perhaps the most powerful description of the entire created order praising God is the song of the three men in the apocryphal part of the Book of Daniel (vv. 29–68). Among the elements which are portrayed there as blessing the Lord and singing his praises are the sun and moon, the stars of heaven, all rain and dew, the winds, fire and heat, winter cold and summer heat, dews and snows, light and darkness, ice and cold, frosts and snows, lightning and clouds, the earth, mountains and hills, all things that grow, springs, seas and rivers, whales and all creatures that move in the waters, all birds of the air, all beasts and cattle and finally the sons of men.

This idea of the whole of creation united in praising God underlies much medieval spirituality. It is the subject matter of a poem that has been described as the most perfect utterance of modern religious sentiment, the 'Canticle of the Creatures', which was composed towards the end of his life by St Francis of Assisi, and is probably known to most of us primarily in the form of the hymn 'All creatures of our God and King'. It is worth quoting a version which more accurately captures the original words of the man who was justly recognised by the Pope in 1980 as the patron saint of ecology:

All praise be yours, my Lord, through all that you have
    made
  And first my lord Brother Sun,
  Who brings the day; and light you give to us through him
How beautiful is he, how radiant in all his splendour!
  Of you, Most High, he bears the likeness.
All praise be yours, my Lord, through Brothers Wind and
    Air,
  And fair and stormy, all the weather's moods,
  By which you cherish all that you have made.
All praise be yours, my Lord, through Brother Fire,
  Through whom you brighten up the night.
  How beautiful is he, how gay! Full of power and strength
All praise be yours, my Lord, through Sister Earth, our
    Mother,
  Who feeds us in her sovereignty and produces
  Various fruits with coloured flowers and herbs.[6]

The relationship between God and nature is portrayed in the Old Testament as being mutual and reciprocal. We have encountered plenty of instances of the natural world praising God but what about examples of his response? There is in fact one fascinating and extraordinary passage in the Book of Hosea which seems to describe inert physical elements engaged in a kind of reciprocal dialogue with one another and with the Lord:

And in that day, says the Lord,
  I will answer the heavens
  and they shall answer the earth;
and the earth shall answer the grain, the wine and the oil,
  and they shall answer Jezreel. (Hos. 2:21, 22)

The German Old Testament scholar Klaus Koch has suggested that this passage expresses a view of God that comes close to panentheism, that is, that he is to be found within

41

nature and is not wholly separate and removed from it. Koch sees such a panentheistic view of God as being a much truer reflection of the Old Testament message than the radically transcendent Deity of later Christian tradition. It has to be said that his argument rests very considerably on this one text. But it certainly ties in with the popular medieval idea of the great chain of being in which God was seen as being linked to all his creation through a dynamic relationship which was not all one way. Dionysius the Areopagite, the sixth-century Neoplatonist whose writings had such a formative influence on medieval mysticism, saw 'a perpetual circle for the Good, from the Good, in the Good and to the Good'. In recent times this way of thinking about the cosmos has received a powerful boost from the work of biologists, who increasingly talk of chains and cycles and in particular from James Lovelock's Gaia thesis which sees the whole world as a living organism bound together by reciprocal ties of dependency. It has also been given new theological credibility by the work of process theologians who tend to be strongly panentheistic in their view of God, seeing him not as purely and simply to be found in and equated with nature (the pantheist position) but rather as penetrating the whole cosmos while still to some extent standing outside it. This break from traditional Christian thinking about God, which has tended to stress his radical transcendence and separation from the world, has clear ecological implications. It may well also be much more biblical.

Perhaps one of the most fruitful and suggestive images we can use to picture this dynamic and reciprocal relationship between God and nature is that of the dance of creation. It is strongly suggested in several passages in the Old Testament which speak of inanimate physical objects like mountains and trees taking on animal characteristics and moving around in a mixture of joy and trembling in the presence of the Lord. The fourth verse of Psalm 114 talks of mountains skipping like rams and hills like lambs. In similar vein is that passage from Isaiah that has become the basis for a catchy contemporary chorus:

For you shall go out in joy,
    and be led forth in peace;
the mountains and the hills before you
    shall break forth into singing,
    and all the trees of the field shall clap their hands.
                  (Isa. 55:12)

The dance of creation was a common theme in popular medieval piety. The carol 'Tomorrow shall be my dancing day' was often sung in parish churches and cathedrals around Christmas time. There is a fine late-sixteenth-century poem by Sir John Davies entitled 'Orchestra, or a Poem of Dancing' which expresses the idea very well:

Dancing, bright lady, then began to be
When the first seeds whereof the world did spring,
The fire air earth and water did agree
By Love's persuasion, nature's might king,
To leave their first discorded combating
And in a dance such measure to observe
And all the world their motion should preserve.

Since when they still are carried in a round,
And changing come one in another's place;
Yet do they neither mingle nor confound,
But every one doth keep the bounded space
Wherein the dance doth bid it turn or trace.
The wondrous miracle doth Love devise,
For dancing is love's proper exercise.

Or if this all, which round about we see,
As idle Morpheus some sick brains hath taught,
Of individual notes compacted be,
How was this goodly architecture wrought?
Or by what means were they together brought?
They err that say they did concur by chance;
Love made them meet in a well-ordered dance.

In a curious and intriguing way this dance theme fits well with the findings of quantum physics that sub-atomic particles are in a state of constant motion, neither entirely random nor wholly determined but involving a delicate and beautifully balanced interplay of chance and necessity. It also fits with the process theologians' view of God luring all his creatures by a persuasive love rather than coercing and cajoling them. The idea of the dance of creation is one that we would do well to recover from its biblical and medieval roots if we are to restore the Green heart of Christianity. It is, of course, a strong motif in eastern religions, particularly in Hinduism where Shiva is regarded as the Lord of the Dance of Creation, the one who maintains the cosmos in life and who is also the presence contained in nature. Perhaps Sydney Carter could be persuaded to write a further verse to his marvellous and justly popular song 'Lord of the Dance' which would portray the cosmic Christ inviting animals and birds, together with the stones and the rocks, to join in his life-giving dance.

Another concept which we could usefully recover is that of the music of the spheres, with God as the composer and conductor – in the American Unitarian hymnwriter John White Chadwick's phrase, the 'Eternal Ruler of the ceaseless round of circling planets singing on their way'. This theme has been taken up recently by the distinguished biologist and Anglican theologian, A. R. Peacocke, who speaks of God as being 'like a composer who, beginning with an arrangement of notes in an apparently simple tune, elaborates and expands it into a fugue by a variety of devices of fragmentation and reassociation'.[7] There is a strongly Platonic element in this kind of imagery but it is also soundly scriptural and has long had an honoured place in Christian spirituality. In 1712 the opening verses of Psalm 19, which begins 'The heavens declare the glory of God; and the firmament sheweth his handiwork' (AV), gave Joseph Addison the inspiration for one of the most beautiful hymns in the English language.

> The spacious firmament on high,
> With all the blue ethereal sky,
> And spangled heavens, a shining frame,
> Their great Original proclaim.
> The unwearied sun, from day to day,

Does his creator's power display,
And publishes to every land
The work of an almighty hand.

Soon as the evening shades prevail,
The moon takes up the wondrous tale,
And nightly to the listening earth
Repeats the story of her birth;
While all the stars that round her burn,
And all the planets, in their turn,
Confirm the tidings, as they roll,
And spread the truth from pole to pole.

What though in solemn silence all
Move round the dark terrestrial ball?
What though no real voice or sound
Amidst their radiant orbs be found?
In reason's ear they all rejoice,
And utter forth a glorious voice,
For ever singing, as they shine,
'The hand that made us is divine'.

A few years after Addison wrote that poem the New England evangelical divine, Jonathan Edwards, produced a remarkable book, *Images or Shadows of Divine Things*, which gave a new dimension to images like the dance of creation and the music of the spheres. Building on the scientific theory of gravity, he portrayed the entire cosmos as locked together in a mutual process of love:

> The whole material world is preserved by gravity or attraction, or the mutual tendency of all bodies to each other. One part of the universe is hereby made beneficial to another; the beauty, harmony and order, regular progress, life and motion, and in short all the well-being of the whole frame depends on it. This is a type of love or charity in the spiritual world.[8]

For Edwards the force pulling everything together was the love of God. This was also an idea that ran through theology in the Middle Ages long before that celebrated apple had descended on Isaac Newton's head and the force of gravity was discovered. In her magisterial work, *L'Esprit de la Philosophie Médiévale*, Etienne Gilson writes that in the medieval mind:

> the physical world, created by God for his glory, is operated from within by a sort of blind love which moves it towards its author, and each being, each activity of each being, depends, at every moment, for both its existence and its efficiency, upon an omnipotent will which conserves it.[9]

In many ways this is a perfect expression of the Christian doctrine of continuous creation which stresses that God's creativity is not limited to a once for all burst of frenzied activity in the first six days of history but shows itself constantly in the sustaining and nurturing of all that exists and in an unending process of new creation.

The doctrine of continuous creation is well established in classical Christian tradition and has solid foundations in both the Old and New Testaments:

> The Lord is the everlasting God,
>   the Creator of the ends of the earth.
> He does not faint or grow weary,
>   his understanding is unsearchable. (Isa. 40:28)

> Jesus answered them, 'My Father is working still, and I am working'. (John 5:17)

There has unfortunately been a strong tendency for churches, particularly in the West, to concentrate so much on creation as a historic event at the beginning of time that they lose sight of this continuing aspect. This has not happened in the eastern Orthodox churches where there has always been a much greater stress on creation as a continuous process. However current trends in western science and theology may well help to correct this imbalance. Indeed to some extent it has already been corrected by the acceptance on the part of all but the most fundamentalist and obscurantist churches of the theory of evolution. For a long time Darwin's discovery that life as we know it on the earth gradually evolved rather than arrived ready-made in a perfect and complete state was thought to be antipathetic to Christian belief. Most theologians now recognise that it in fact gives a much more important role to God as continuous creator of the world than the old idea that he made everything in six days and then sat back and did nothing.

The new science of quantum physics also gives a welcome boost to the idea of continuous creation. The old Newtonian idea of the universe as an intricate piece of machinery that ticked away went well with the Deist idea of God as the watchmaker who started it all going and then watched it unwind. Now scientists have given us a picture of the universe which is much less mechanistic and determined, much more open-ended and still in the process of evolution. It is not a wholly random picture – there is a unified field underlying everything but within it individual atoms and quarks seem to have great freedom and to be continually facing a range of options. In Christian terms this fits well with the doctrine of continuous creation and with the idea that physical as well as human matter is given free will and is constantly being offered by God a range of possibilities.

Both evolution and quantum physics have profoundly influenced the development of process thought in the twentieth century. As its name implies, the central tenet of this school of philosophers and theologians is that God's relationship with the world is best seen as a constant process which goes on all the time and is without beginning or end. For process thinkers, indeed, it is impossible to conceive of God other than as engaged in continuous creation and interacting with his creatures – it is his whole nature to create and have relationships. Significantly the language that leading process philosophers like A. N. Whitehead and Charles Hartshorne have used comes very close to what we have already encountered in Joseph Addison, Jonathan Edwards and the medieval mystics. They talk of God luring the world, persuading it by love rather than coercing it, and also of his being influenced by it. They have a strong sense of his presence in nature and of the dynamism and movement that earlier generations expressed through the image of the dance of creation.

If modern science can assist us to see a much greater continuous interaction between God and all his creation, it may also help to reintroduce an element of mystery and wonder into our view of nature. At first sight this may seem an unlikely role for science, given its traditional position as the great debunker of mystery and prime opponent of the relgious outlook. It is true that in the past scientists have often sought to explain everything rationally so that God became the God of the gaps, only there to account for the inexplicable, his scope further and further reduced until he could finally be explained away altogether. But in recent years a remarkable transformation has occurred in scientific thinking. Scientists have been much struck not just by the order and symmetry of the natural world but by its awesome beauty and mystery. John Polkinghorne, the physicist turned Anglican priest, has written much about the development of this new kind of natural theology. He sees it as 'a rational response to the strange and beautiful world science discloses, with its feel of "more than meets the eye".'[10] This recalls Albert Einstein's sense that something deeply hidden has to be behind things. Increasingly those working at the frontiers of biology, physics and astronomy feel a sense of awe and wonder at what they are discovering and confronting and turn to the language of poetry rather than scientific discourse to describe it. This experience is not necessarily turning them into Christians but it is making them more conscious of the power of the numinous and more religious in the broadest sense of the word.

These new stirrings in the scientific world open up interesting prospects for a revival of some of the classical proofs for belief in God and of traditional natural theology. They point the way for a much more ecological and holistic view of the relationship between the Creator of the world and all his creatures. They also revolutionise our view of physical matter, suggesting that what we have seen as static and inanimate is in fact charged with dynamic activity. As Donald Mackay writes in his book, *Science, Chance and Providence*:

> Ask a physicist to describe what he finds as he probes deeper and deeper into the fine structure of our solid world, and he will tell you a story of an increasingly dynamic character. Instead of a frozen stillness, he discovers a buzz of activity that seems to intensify as the magnification increases.[11]

One part of the Christian Church has always held to such a view of matter, seeing it as being charged directly with divine energy. Expressing the eastern Orthodox position Professor Paul Evdokimov has written that 'matter is never inert . . . it is animated by a concentrated and, as it were, a dormant energy'.[12] The foundations of this idea rest on the biblical passages which have been quoted in this chapter and also on the doctrine propounded by the Greek Fathers of the distinction between the essence and energies of God. Heavily influenced by Platonism, they felt that God as the supreme good could not be directly in contact with the changing and corruptible world of physical matter. Yet they also had a strong incarnational sense that God through Jesus Christ had chosen to reveal and identify himself wholly in and with the physical and material. They also wanted strongly to express their sense that the whole universe reflected and responded to the glory of its Creator and sustainer. In order to preserve both the transcendence and the immanence of God they developed a distinction between his essence, which lay beyond all human experience and was wholly spiritual, and his energies in which all life and matter participated. For them matter was indeed God's will and energy made palpable. Far from being corrupt and evil, it became mysterious and deeply sacred.

This sacramental attitude towards the world of matter has never left the eastern Orthodox churches. It explains why they have a much more holistic perspective than most western Christians and have never really entertained the idea of human domination over nature. We badly need to recover this sense of God's energy being present in inanimate as well as in organic nature. The theology and practice of contemporary Orthodox churches can certainly point us in the right direction. So also can the writings of some in our own western Catholic tradition. The great French biologist and theologian, Pierre Teilhard de Chardin, saw matter as the divine milieu, charged with creative power. For him the Christian doctrine of the Incarnation made all physical things sacred. Seeing God as both the immanent motor of evolution and the transcendent pull of all creative forces, he held that far from existing to be dominated and used by man the true destiny of nature was to carry man up to God. In his great hymn to matter he prays: 'Raise me up then, matter, to those heights, through struggle and separation and death; raise me up until, at long last, it becomes possible for me in perfect chastity to embrace the universe.'[13]

The sacramental approach to nature of Teilhard de Chardin and the eastern Orthodox Church; new insights gained from quantum physics and process philosophy; the increasing sense of awe and wonder with which scientists gaze on the universe; recovering traditional Christian themes like the great chain of being, the dance of creation and the music of the spheres: all of these may help us to see, as the psalmists and prophets saw nearly three thousand years ago, that God is engaged in a continuous and reciprocal relationship with all his creation. Perhaps we can be helped too by the Holy Spirit, that mysterious power which still moves across the face of the waters just as she stirs deep down in all our hearts. Few people have had such a sense of the workings of the Spirit in the world of nature as the nineteenth-century Jesuit priest and poet Gerard Manley Hopkins. I can think of no better text for leading us back to this neglected aspect of God's greenness than his poem 'God's Grandeur':

The world is charged with the grandeur of God,
   It will flame out, like shining from shook foil;
   It gathers to a greatness, like the ooze of oil
Crushed. Why do men then now not reck his rod?
Generations have trod, have trod, have trod;
   And all is seared with trade; bleared, smeared with toil;

And wears man's smudge and shares man's smell: the soil
Is bare now, nor can foot feel, being shod.

And for all this, nature is never spent;
   There lives the dearest freshness deep down things;
And though the last lights off the black West went
   Oh, morning, at the brown brink eastward, springs –
Because the Holy Ghost over the bent
   World broods with warm breast and with ah! bright wings.

3

The fall of nature
The whole creation has been groaning in travail

So far we have looked at two ideas supposedly rooted in Christianity which have proved highly damaging to the environment: the dominion of man over the rest of creation; and the stripping away from nature of all mystery and sanctity. It has, I hope, been clearly demonstrated that the way in which both these themes have been developed in the West is totally at odds with the message of the Bible and the teaching of the early Church. In respect at least of these two charges that are commonly laid against it, Christianity can be declared not guilty and shown to be eco-friendly.

Now we come to a more difficult and complex doctrine, that of the fall. To many outsiders, and to not a few believers as well, it seems the most unattractive feature of the whole Christian faith, hanging gloomily over everything like a funeral shroud and preventing any real celebration of the goodness of God's creation. For those concerned about the natural environment there is something particularly unattractive about the doctrine of the fall. They argue, with some justice, that Christians have stressed the fall of the natural world much more than the fall of humans and that as a result it has not just been deprived of its sacred character but rendered positively evil and demonic. This low view of fallen nature, it is held, has greatly encouraged exploitative and dismissive attitudes towards the world around us and helped to bring about the ecological crisis that we are now facing.

There is certainly no doubt that a stress on the fallen aspect of creation has long been a feature of western Christianity. As Professor Basil Willey points out in *The Seventeenth-Century Background*:

From the earliest days of man there had of course been evil forces in Nature to be feared and propitiated; but during the Christian centuries 'Nature' had, in quite a special sense, been consigned to the Satanic order . . . The sense which above all marks the Christian consciousness, of sin in man and of imperfection in Nature, expressed itself in a virtual dualism, the Satanic forces being as real as the divine.[1]

This kind of thinking is very clearly exemplified in John Milton's ingenious explanation for the traditional winter setting of the Christmas story in his 'Ode on the Morning of Christ's Nativity' (1629):

> It was the winter wild
> While the Heaven-born child
>   All meanly wrapped in the rude manger lies;
> Nature in awe to Him
> Had doffed her gaudy trim
>   With her great Master so to sympathize;
> It was no season then for her
> To wanton with the sun, her lusty paramour.
>
> Only with speeches fair
> She woos the gentle air
>   To hide her guilty front with innocent snow,
> And on her naked shame,
> Pollute with sinful blame,
>   The saintly veil of maiden white to throw,
> Confounded that her Maker's eyes
> Should look so near upon her foul deformities.

The idea that the natural world is full of naked shame and sinful blame is deeply embedded in the western mind. In his book, *Theology of Nature*, Professor George Hendry attributes the comparatively late development of natural science in Europe to the fact that Christianity 'had turned it into a realm of darkness as well as malice'.[2] Professor Dantine has argued that 'the popular doctrine of the "fallen creation" clouds the clear insight that evil is always caused by the responsible acts of men . . . The word about the "fallen creation" unintentionally renders the whole cosmos demonic and obscures our perception of the tasks of man.'[3]

In the last few years there have been several attempts to establish a more environment-friendly and life-affirming Christianity. At its most radical this has involved virtually jettisoning altogether the traditional doctrines of the fall and original sin. In his best-selling book, *Original Blessing*, the American Dominican Matthew Fox argues that we should let go of what he calls the 'Fall/Redemption' tradition that has been dominant in western Christianity since Augustine and go back to the creation-centred spirituality of the Old Testament and the early Fathers. He finds it curious that while 99 per cent of Christians know all about original sin, only a handful think in terms of original blessing and the goodness of God's creation.

We certainly need constantly to be reminded of those often forgotten words that conclude the creation story in the first chapter of Genesis, 'and God saw everything that he had made, and behold it was very good'. Matthew Fox and others are right to lead us back to the creation-centred spirituality which, as we have already seen, is so clear a feature of both the Bible and the early Church. Contemporary feminist theologians have also done a valuable service in rediscovering another important Christian concept that has been buried by centuries of concentration on the fall and the sinfulness of nature – the fertility and goodness of the earth. This was a point that was grasped especially clearly by the great twelfth-century mystic Hildegarde of Bingen who noted joyfully that 'holy persons draw themselves to all that is earthly'.[4] We are apt to forget that the great Christian virtue of humility means first and foremost being close to the earth and has much more to do with being in tune with nature than with creeping servitude of the Uriah Heep variety.

But can we really dispense with the doctrine of the fall? Quite apart from the fact that it is clearly spelt out in both the Old and the New Testaments, does not the idea that there is something unsatisfactory and imperfect both in nature and in human nature square with our own experience of life? Do we not feel a sense of frustration as well as a sense of wonder as we contemplate ourselves and the world around us, an ambiguity that is well expressed in one of the marvellous prayers written by Lord MacLeod of Fuinary for the Iona Community:

Almighty God, Creator: the morning is yours, rising into fullness. The summer is yours, dipping into autumn. Eternity is yours, dipping into time. The vibrant grasses, the scent of flowers, the lichen on the rocks, the tang of seaweed, all are yours. Gladly we live in this garden of your creating.

But creation is not enough. Always in the beauty, the foreshadowing of decay. The lambs frolicking careless: so soon to be led off to slaughter. Nature red and scarred as well as lush and green. In the garden also: always the thorn. Creation is not enough.

Almighty God, Redeemer: the sap of life in our bones and being is yours lifting us to ecstasy. But always in the beauty, the tang of sin, in our own consciences. The dry lichen of sins long dead, but seared on the mind. In the garden that is each of us, always the thorn.[5]

The idea that the natural world, like human nature, is not all that it might be is an essential part of Christian doctrine, just as it is an inescapable fact of life. It is first expressed in the Bible just after the two creation accounts at the beginning of the Book of Genesis. There the fall of nature is referred to twice – first at the end of the story of Adam and Eve's expulsion from the Garden of Eden and secondly at the beginning of the story of Noah and the flood. On both occasions it is linked directly to the fall of man because of his sin.

And to Adam [God] said:
'Because you have listened to the voice of your wife,
    and have eaten of the tree
    of which I commanded you,

"you shall not eat of it,"
cursed is the ground because of you.' (Gen. 3:17)

The Lord saw that the wickedness of man was great in the earth, and that every imagination of the thoughts of his heart was only evil continually. And the Lord was sorry that he had made man on the earth, and it grieved him to his heart. So the Lord said, 'I will blot out man whom I have created from the face of the ground, man and beast and creeping things and birds of the air, for I am sorry that I have made them' . . . And God saw the earth, and behold, it was corrupt; for all flesh had corrupted their way upon the earth. And God said to Noah: 'I have determined to make an end of all flesh; for the earth is filled with violence through them; behold, I will destroy them with the earth.' (Gen. 6:5–7, 12–13)

Both these accounts preserve very clearly the intimate association between humans and other parts of creation that we have seen underlying the theology of the Old Testament. The fall of nature is linked directly with the fall of man. Indeed it is presented as a simple case of cause and effect: it is the fall of man that has led to the fall of nature. This is particularly clear in the first passage where Adam is specifically told 'cursed is the ground because of you'. But it is also the clear message of the second passage as well. Although it talks about 'all flesh' having corrupted the earth it is pretty clear that the real culprit is man. In the words of Bernhard Anderson, Emeritus Professor of Old Testament Theology at Princeton Theological Seminary and a leading authority on the Genesis creation narratives: 'While the animals were affected by the violence and corruption of the earth, there is no suggestion in the Primeval history that they were the source of the violence . . . rather the violence that corrupted "all flesh" is traced to the Creator's noblest creatures'.[6]

In view of this clear biblical teaching it is not surprising that the classical Christian interpretation of the fall of nature has been that it is a direct consequence of human sinfulness. As John Calvin put it, Adam's sin 'perverted the whole order of nature in heaven and on earth'.[7] It is, of course, possible to give a highly ecological slant to this interpretation. It is man who through his violent ways has brought about the terrible punishment that is inflicted on the whole of creation. Humans are directly responsible for shattering the primeval harmony of the world of nature. They have abused the dominion given to them by God over the rest of creation by failing to exercise it in his image as loving stewards, and instead have tried to play the role of the Almighty themselves by ruthlessly exploiting and destroying animals, plants and mineral resources. Such an interpretation squares well with what we know to be the basic cause of the ills that our planet is now suffering, from the depletion of the ozone layer to the destruction of the rain forests, from the virtual wiping out of the elephant population to the loss of hedgerows and woods from our countryside.

A number of Christians down the ages have seen the fall as a highly ecological doctrine which points to the destructive impact of human beings on the rest of nature. The Puritan radical Gerrard Winstanley argued that at the beginning of time 'there was an evenness between man and all creatures, an evenness between man and his Maker the Lord, the Spirit'. This initial harmony was broken, however, when man started to look on other creatures as objects and specifically when he began regarding the earth as his property, buying and selling parcels of land and saying 'this is mine' about something which was in reality a common treasury. It was this that brought about the curse which manifested itself in strife between creatures:

> For when the Father made creation, he made all elements to uphold one another in righteousness, and one creature to preserve another, therefore it was all very good. But this rising up of creatures to destroy one another is the curse of which unrighteous man, that is, the Lord of the creatures, hath brought upon the creation.[8]

A similar approach to the doctrine of the fall can be found

in modern eastern Orthodox theology. Professor Paul Evdokimov writes that:

> It is man endowed with freedom of choice who abdicates his royal dignity and thus disorganises the pre-established order, as soon as he no longer consciously affirms the 'bond of love' with nature. Being thrown out of joint like this, nature is 'dehumanised' and this explains why it stands outside of Good and Evil . . . In its cosmic repercussions, the Fall has perverted not only the initial relations between God and man, but also those between man and the Cosmos.[9]

Such interpretations are encouraged by the garden setting in which the drama of the fall takes place. Humans, according to the older creation story in the second chapter of Genesis, are put into the world to till the soil and to look after the earth in a co-operative endeavour with God. It is when they try to go it alone and to lord it over the rest of creation that things go wrong. The biblical account of the fall could indeed be read as a story of what happens when Adam ceases organic husbandry and introduces intensive methods of agriculture. There have been some ingenious attempts to explain the story of Adam and Eve's fall from the Garden of Eden and God's cursing of the earth in terms of the transition of the human species from a nomadic life of gathering fruits and berries to a more settled and laborious existence based on agriculture and keeping animals for food. It is certainly significant that in the Garden of Eden vegetarianism is portrayed as the norm among both animals and humans. Man's carnivorous instincts only come to the fore after the fall and his harmonious existence with the animal kingdom is only shattered after the flood:

> And God blessed Noah and his sons, and said to them, 'Be fruitful and multiply, and fill the earth. The fear of you and the dread of you shall be upon every beast of the earth, and upon every bird of the air, upon everything that creeps on the ground and all the fish of the sea; into your hand

they are delivered. Every moving thing that lives shall be food for you; and as I gave you the green plants, I give you everything.' (Gen. 9:2)

The accounts of the fall and the flood in Genesis seem to reflect some of the most important transitions in the evolution of the human species – the shift from vegetarianism to meat-eating, the change from going out and gathering the fruits of nature to the hard physical effort of tilling the soil to grow crops, the increasing differentiation between humans and animals as the latter became reared for food. It appears that humans were originally largely vegetarian, surviving on fruits, grains and plants gathered largely by women. It also seems to have been women who first made the discovery that seeds of certain plants saved from one season to the next and planted at a particular time could produce food-yielding crops and thus made the breakthrough from the nomadic life of the hunter to the settled life of the farmer. This may even give some significance to the fact that it is Eve who gets the blame for tasting the forbidden fruit.

One of the main purposes of the whole extended creation story in the early chapters of the Bible was to explain to the ancient Israelites why they found themselves having to work hard in their fields all day and were not able to just sit back and enjoy life. In more general terms it addresses the question why the human race as a whole finds itself in a situation of toil and travail rather than of rest, and speaks to our sense that all is not as well as it might be, or perhaps as it once was, in the relations between humans and the natural environment. The implication is that it is we who are responsible for this disharmony and the drudgery which follows from it. Certainly this seems to be the message of the Lord's remark to Adam when he curses the ground:

> in toil shall you eat it all the days of your life;
> thorns and thistles it shall bring forth to you;
> and you shall eat the plants of the field.
> In the sweat of your face

you shall eat bread
till you return to the ground. (Gen. 3:17–19)

It is almost as if the world of nature has responded to its
rough and callous treatment at the hands of humans by prov-
ing hostile and unmanageable. That is certainly how Gerrard
Winstanley saw it in the mid-seventeenth century. He felt
that when man fell out with his maker, the creatures fell out
with him and became his enemies and opponents. The same
thought underlies Ralph Waldo Emerson's poem 'Blight':

The injured elements say, 'Not in us';
And night and day, ocean and continent,
Fire, plant and mineral say 'Not in us':
And haughtily return us stare for stare.
For we invade them impiously for gain;
We devastate them unreligiously
And coldly ask their pottage, not their love.

However this is not quite what the Bible says. It does not
portray a rebellion by nature against man but rather a direct
curse by God on the whole of creation because of the specific
faults of one part of it. This idea that the earth is cursed as
a punishment on man recurs at several points throughout the
Old Testament. It is a particular theme of the prophets Isaiah
and Jeremiah who see the sins of the people of Israel bringing
forth drought and other natural disasters.

The earth shall be utterly laid waste and utterly despoiled;
  for the Lord has spoken this word.
The earth mourns and withers,
    the world languishes and withers;
    the heavens languish together with the earth.
The earth lies polluted
    under its inhabitants;
for they have transgressed the laws,
    violated the statutes,
    broken the everlasting covenant. (Isa. 24:3–5)

I looked on the earth, and lo, it was waste and void;
    and to the heavens, and they had no light.
I looked on the mountains, and lo, they were quaking,
    and all the hills moved to and fro.
I looked, and lo, there was no man,
    and all the birds of the air had fled.
I looked, and lo, the fruitful land was a desert,
    and all its cities were laid in ruins
      before the Lord, before his fierce anger. (Jer. 4:23–26)

Jeremiah portrays drought as a punishment from God on his rebellious and sinful people; but he describes in very moving terms how it also affects the innocent wild animals who have done nothing to deserve such an affliction:

Because of the ground which is dismayed,
    since there is no rain on the land,
the farmers are ashamed,
    they cover their heads.
Even the hind in the field forsakes her newborn calf
    because there is no grass.
The wild asses stand on the bare heights,
    they pant for air like jackals;
their eyes fail
    because there is no herbage. (Jer. 14:4–6)

These verses could be interpreted as having a very Green message. As we know only too well, drought and 'desert-ification' are often directly caused by human activities such as cutting down trees, over-intensive farming and poor irrigation. Living where he did in a place where fertile land merged into desert, Jeremiah must have been well aware of how easy it was to destroy the thin layer of top soil and create dust bowls. Possibly he had this in mind when he wrote so powerfully about the effects of drought on both humans and animals. His particularly moving evocation of the suffering of the wild asses also highlights one of the major problems about interpreting the fall of nature as a response by God to human sin. It is quite inconsistent with the dominant Old Testament

61

view of the Almighty as the Lord of creation, concerned with sustaining everything that he has made. Why on earth should the rest of creation be made to suffer because of the sin of just one part of it? It seems monstrously unfair to inflict on innocent nature a punishment which only humans deserve.

It may well be that the story of the fall has something to tell us about our responsibility as humans for despoiling nature. But the idea that animals, plants and the very elements of earth and water are all punished by God because of something man has done is surely unacceptable. It takes us back to our besetting sin of anthropocentrism, suggesting that everything that happens in the world, both good and ill, can somehow be traced back to a human cause. Many Christians have held to the view that natural disasters such as earthquakes and floods are a visitation from God on human sin. Charles Moule, the distinguished Cambridge New Testament scholar, for example, asks whether:

> on those occasions when man is cruelly hurt and destroyed by calamities which are contrary, as we feel sure, to the purpose and will of God, it may not be ultimately part of an almost infinitely long and subtle chain of cause and effect into which man's disobedience has entered.[10]

In the last few years some Christians have seen a rather shorter and less subtle chain of cause and effect linking sexual promiscuity with the AIDS virus. This way of thinking is surely to be rejected vehemently, not least because it posits a cruel and spiteful Deity far removed from the figure of the suffering servant, the sacrificial victim and the One overflowing with love whom Christians worship as God incarnate.

The idea that 'fallen' nature represents God's punishment on human sin is not only arrogantly anthropocentric; it also flies in the face of logic and the facts of evolution. What about all the earthquakes and volcanic eruptions and other natural disasters that occurred on the planet long before *Homo sapiens* arrived on the scene? We surely cannot see them as some kind of future punishment for human misdemeanour. And what about all the mutations and disasters that continuously afflict the animal and plant kingdoms but have no impact at all on the human world? We need to find some explanation for the manifest disharmony and suffering in nature that is independent of human sin.

There are several ways of interpreting the doctrine of the fall which preserve the sense that there is profound ambiguity and imperfection in the world of nature but do not fall into the anthropocentric trap of putting all the responsibility for this on to the shoulders of man. One is to follow the biblical stress on the powerful forces of chaos which constantly threaten the order and stability of creation. This is a theme which has received considerable attention among Old Testament theologians in the twentieth century, thanks largely to the pioneering work of the great German scholar Herman Gunkel. In his seminal work, *Creation and Chaos*, published in 1895, he used the term *Chaoskampf* to describe the dominant theme of the opening chapters of the Old Testament. Classical Christian theology has portrayed God as creating the world out of nothing – *ex nihilo*. The Genesis creation stories, however, show him rather as creating it out of chaos, represented particularly by the element of water which the ancient Israelites seem to have feared more than any other.

At the beginning of creation the Holy Spirit is pictured as moving over the face of the primeval waters. God goes on to divide the waters from the waters, an action explicable in terms of Hebrew cosmology which envisaged the earth as floating on water and the heavens as being erected as a kind of giant umbrella to hold back the water which surrounds the cosmos. While the watery forces of chaos are reined in and tamed by God they are never completely eliminated or subdued. The story of the flood shows them returning. The Israelites never felt able to put the sea totally under God's sovereignty. The forces of chaos remain an ever-present threat in the New Testament until the Book of Revelation triumphantly declares that at the new creation there will be no more sea.

It is interesting that one of the most exciting areas of contemporary science is chaology, the name given to the study of the apparently random disorder which seems to lie at the heart of all matter. There are striking similarities between what those engaged in this new discipline are finding and the Old Testament view of the world as having been created out of chaos and given shape and direction by God. One of the most striking results of chaology so far has been the production of enhanced computer graphics which show a remarkable beauty and symmetry being fashioned out of the underlying disorder. Is not this what the authors of Genesis were also telling us when they wrote of the Spirit moving across the face of the primeval waters and God dividing the waters from the waters? It may well be that this way of interpreting the 'fallenness' of nature gains ground in the coming years.

Another rather similar way of interpreting the doctrine of the fall of nature is to see it as pointing to the unavoidable collisions that occur in a physical system that is in constant motion and where millions of highly charged particles are rushing around. To extend the image taken up in Chapter 2, if all of creation is indeed engaged in a great dance it is inevitable that from time to time feet get trodden on and people get bumped into. This interpretation of the doctrine of the fall was strongly canvassed by the Anglican cleric Austin Farrer. In his *Love Almighty and Ills Unlimited* he argued that without an element of disorder and conflict the world would simply be a machine, a magically self-arranged garden:

> Gone would be that enormous vitality of force, which makes every system or concentration of energy to radiate over the whole field of space, every living kind to propagate without restraint, and, in a word, every living creature to absolutize itself, so far as in it lies, and to be the whole world, if it can. It cannot, admittedly; and why? Because of interference by a million rivals, all equally reckless in their own vitality. Eliminate the mutual interferences, and gone, equally, will be the drama of an existence continually at stake, of a being which has to be achieved and held, of the unexpected and the improvised.[11]

This kind of approach to the fall of nature has certain clear strengths. It reminds us of the ambiguity of creation, as the Iona Community prayer puts it: 'nature red and scarred as well as lush and green'. It offers an explanation for natural disasters that does not introduce human sin as a casual agent. It does, of course, put a limitation on God's power, which goes against traditional notions of his omnipotence and suggests that there is a sphere which even he cannot completely master. It also seems to leave us all at the mercy of the wayward elements. There is presumably nothing to stop chaos returning and ruling again. Indeed perhaps that is exactly what will happen as the ozone layer disappears and the greenhouse effect melts the polar ice caps and raises the level of the oceans. Once again, it will be the sea that destroys the earth.

There is however another way of interpreting the doctrine of the fall which gives us grounds for a rather more hopeful view of the future of our planet. What if the 'original sin' that human and non-human creation share together is not so much a definite attribute or action like pride or turning away from God but more a general state of imperfection and immaturity? Could it be that the Garden of Eden is indeed a symbol of the perfect and harmonious existence that God intends for all his creatures but that it is a goal which we are moving towards by his grace and not a primeval paradise from which we were kicked out long ago? Does it not in fact properly come at the end of the human story rather than at the beginning?

This approach fits in well with the doctrine of continuous creation which was explored in the previous chapter. It has been taken up by a number of modern theologians, most notably perhaps Jürgen Moltmann, Professor of Systematic Theology at the University of Tübingen in West German. In many of his writings he has argued for creation to be viewed not as a past event, something that is final and perfect and over and done with, but as an open-ended process which is still going on. This kind of interpretation has clear ecological implications. As Moltmann writes in his essay, 'Creation as an open system':

Man no longer confronts God's non-human creation as its lord, the creature who was made in the image of God; together with all other things, he also stands in the Becoming of the still open, uncompleted process of creation. Creation is then not so much a *factum* but a *fieri*. This leads to a new interpretation of man's destiny in creation; and 'subdue the earth' cannot be this destiny's final word.[12]

Pierre Teilhard de Chardin had much the same perspective, arguing that 'nature is the equivalent of becoming'. As a biologist he saw evolution as the central feature of both spiritual and physical life with Jesus Christ being the Omega point towards which everything is moving. Imperfection and frustration had not come into the world as the result of a historic 'fall' event. Rather they were part of the condition of things from the very beginning. But they do not represent our destiny and God's ultimate purposes for his creation. We can only accept the disturbing and disquieting aspects of nature because 'we know by faith that we are, as it were, at the base of a cone'.[13]

This picture of the world as being in a perpetual state of becoming rather than as having been perfectly formed and completed at the moment of creation is also very much in harmony with modern scientific theory. The principle of evolution suggests a world that is constantly developing and open to the future, not a closed system fixed for all time as it is now. In 1981 two process theologians, John Cobb and Charles Birch, published *The Liberation of Life: from cell to community*, in which evolution is pictured as a series of 'falls upward'. The authors explain this phrase by saying that it 'identifies the occurrence of a new level of order and freedom bought at the price of suffering'.[14] Each new step up the evolutionary ladder brings new dangers and an increased potential for suffering just as it brings new positive possibilities as well. Every time a species evolves, there is an increase in freedom and in consciousness and therefore a greater risk and a greater propensity to feel despair as well as happiness. The point was well made by Søren Kierkegaard in his classic study *From Sickness unto Death*: 'With every increase in the degree of consciousness, and in proportion to that increase, the intensity of despair increases: the more consciousness, the more intense the despair.'[15]

Quantum physics may also help to show how the 'fallen-ness' of creation manifests itself in the natural as well as the human world. It portrays the tiny particles of matter that make up the cosmos being in a constant state of motion and perpetually confronted with different possibilities. Could it be that they sometimes take the 'wrong direction' and that the signs of disordered and disjointed nature from the cancer cell to the earthquake are the result of freedom being abused by God's non-human creatures, just as so much human misery is the result of our abuse of his most precious gift to us? It is not a matter of God using nature as an agent to punish sinful humanity but of his giving freedom to all his creatures. In the words of John Polkinghorne, 'In his great act of creation God allows the physical world to be itself . . . in that independence which is Love's gift of freedom to the one beloved.'[16]

From this perspective the doctrine of the fall leads not to a contemplation of the sorry state of the world now compared to what it once was but to a sense of frustration about what we are compared to what we might be. This kind of approach characterised the writings of many of the early Fathers of the Church. It is perhaps most clearly evident in the thought of Irenaeus, Bishop of Lyons, in the late second century, who argued that creation was an evolutionary process involving two distinct stages. In the beginning creatures were made in the image of God but only gradually were they being brought to his likeness. For Irenaeus all of creation, including human beings, is as yet in a state of immaturity and perfection lies in the future rather than in some past golden age. The same idea underlay the notion of deification developed by the Greek Fathers who held that the natural destiny of all creatures is to rise up towards God and be at one with him.

This kind of forward-looking evolutionary approach can also be found in the Bible. The Old Testament prophets were well aware that the world is not all that it might be – that there is violence and disorder both among humans and in the realm of nature. However they did not look back to a golden age before the fall when all was peaceful and harmonious. Rather they looked forward to a time when all would be made perfect and whole by the Messiah sent from God. This was

especially true of Isaiah. I have already quoted those verses
in which he looked forward to a time when the mountains
and hills would break forth into singing and the trees of the
field would clap their hands, when waters would flow in the
wilderness and streams appear in the desert. In another
famous passage he gives an even more striking prophecy of
what will happen when the Messiah comes:

> There shall come forth a shoot from the stump of Jesse,
>   and a branch shall grow out of his roots.
> And the Spirit of the Lord shall rest upon him,
>   the spirit of wisdom and understanding,
>   the spirit of counsel and might,
>   the spirit of knowledge and fear of the Lord.
> And his delight shall be in the fear of the Lord.
> He shall not judge by what his eyes see,
>   or decide by what his ears hear;
> but with righteousness he shall judge the poor,
>   and decide with equity for the meek of the earth;
> and he shall smite the earth with the rod of his mouth,
>   and with the breath of his lips he shall slay the wicked.
> Righteousness shall be the girdle of his waist,
>   and faithfulness the girdle of his loins.
> The wolf shall dwell with the lamb,
>   and the leopard shall lie down with the kid,
> and the calf and the lion and the fatling together
>   and a little child shall lead them.
> The cow and the bear shall feed;
>   their young shall lie down together;
>   and the lion shall eat straw like the ox.
> The sucking child shall play over the hole of the asp,
>   and the weaned child shall put his hand on the adder's
>   den.
> They shall not hurt or destroy
>   in all my holy mountain;
> for the earth shall be full of the knowledge of the Lord
>   as the water covers the sea. (Isa. 11:1–9)

Isaiah's remarkable vision of the harmony that will reign

in the animal kingdom when the rule of righteousness is established in the world is worthy of a brief exegesis. The most interesting commentary on it that I have come across is by the German scholar Otto Kaiser. He points out the obvious relationship between this passage and the description of the primal harmony and vegetarianism in the Garden of Eden at the beginning of Genesis. However in his view it should not be reduced 'to a mere search for security projected back into the primal period. We should rather assume that here we have the expression of a sensibility which is aware of the primal guilt in all life, which can only survive through the death of other life.' He goes on to say that the Isaiah passage can all too easily be dismissed as wishful thinking when in fact, as well as being a direct promise of what will come about in the last days, it is also a call:

> to regain a feeling for the primal vitiation of our lives, to recognize that our own life is always made possible by the sacrifice of other life and is fulfilled only by surrender to other people. The result of this would be a new reverence for life, primarily for the life of other people, and then, by virtue of the unity of all life, reverence also for the life of animals.[17]

In other words it is a strong ecological statement with a very Green message.

The point that Kaiser raises about sacrifice leads us, I think, to another very important truth which is conveyed by the doctrine of the fall. The maintenance and continuation of all forms of life on our planet depends on sacrifice, often indeed on the sacrifice of lives as weaker strains and species surrender to stronger. The Darwinian principle of the survival of the fittest confirmed what had long been clear to many observers of the natural world – that its progress and stability was only achieved at a very considerable cost. In human life as in nature sacrifice and self-surrender are essential for the coherence of the community and the preservation of the species. In the words of the great Victorian divine F. D. Maurice, 'sacrifice lies at the very root of our being; our lives stand upon it; society is held together by it'.[18] For Christians, of course, mention of sacrifice points us immediately to Our Lord's death on the cross, commemorated in the Eucharist. The link between this sacrifice and the sacrifice that is continually going on in the natural and human worlds will be explored in Chapter 4. For now, it is enough to point to the way in which this mysterious and disquieting truth about the basis of all life is expressed in the Christian doctrine of the fall of creation.

There is both a realisation of the constant sacrifice and suffering within the cosmos and a sense of looking forward in expectation, rather than casting longing glances back, in those majestic words which St Paul wrote to the Romans:

> I consider that the sufferings of this present time are not worth comparing with the glory that is to be revealed to us. For the creation waits with eager longing for the revealing of the sons of God; for the creation was subjected to futility, not of its own will but by the will of him who subjected it in hope; because the creation itself will be set free from its bondage to decay and obtain the glorious liberty of the children of God. We know that the whole creation has been groaning in travail together until now; and not only the creation, but we ourselves, who have the first fruits of the Spirit, groan inwardly as we wait for adoption as sons, the redemption of our bodies. (Rom. 8:18–23)

Of all the passages in the Bible that refer to the world of nature none is surely so profound, so mysterious or so relevant to our present ecological crisis as this. It takes up and amplifies the two themes that we have already found in the Old Testament: the interdependence and common destiny of the whole of creation and the special role of humans in liberating and perfecting the non-human world. In particularly graphic and moving terms, Paul portrays us as standing side by side with the rest of creation in our groaning and travail, frustrated and impatient at our imperfections and shortcomings, but waiting expectantly and hopefully for liberty and fulfilment.

As sons and daughters of God, created uniquely in his image, we have a key part to play in establishing the new creation which Jesus Christ has inaugurated.

The word which Paul uses for the subject of this passage, κτισις in Greek, has been translated in many different ways, sometimes to apply only to humans and sometimes to cover all creation. But there is a growing consensus among New Testament scholars that it should properly be taken to mean the sum total of non-human nature, both animate and inanimate. What is particularly striking is the way in which Paul portrays it in human terms, waiting with eager longing and groaning as in the labours of childbirth. His words echo those verses in the Psalms and the prophets which seem to give a life and a voice to mountains and trees and to picture the world of nature responding in an almost human way to God's love and care. But they also go beyond the Old Testament passages in a way that was pointed out around a century ago by the great Anglican theologian Charles Gore:

> In his representation of the present aspects of nature Paul strikes an extraordinarily modern note by exhibiting a deep and real sympathy with nature in her pain from her own point of view. The Psalms can supply examples of a real sympathetic fellowship in the happiness of creation. But here we have, as nowhere else in the Bible – perhaps nowhere in ancient literature – a man who feels with the pain of creation.[19]

The way in which Paul describes the pain and suffering of creation strongly suggests that he held to the view which we have been exploring in this chapter which sees the 'fallen' aspect of nature in terms of immaturity and incompleteness. The Greek word ματαιοτης which Paul uses to describe the present condition of the world has been variously translated as vanity, loss of purpose, frustration and futility (as in the Revised Standard Version quoted above). The New Testament scholar C. E. B. Cranfield is surely right to suggest that it should be taken 'as denoting the ineffectiveness of that which does not attain its goal, the frustration of not being

71

able to fulfill its existence'.[20] The phrase in which it occurs is difficult and puzzling: 'for the creation was subjected to futility not by its own will, but by the will of him who subjected it in hope'. Several commentators have seen it as referring back to the Genesis account of the fall of nature, to Adam's sin and to God's wrath on account of it. But there have also been a number of distinguished New Testament scholars who have given it a very different interpretation. C. H. Dodd, for example, noted that in this passage the material world's subjection to futility is traced 'not, as in some contemporary theories, to the sin of Adam, for whose sake the earth was believed to have been cursed, but vaguely to the will of God, i.e. it is in the nature of things as they are, though not of necessity permanent'.[21] Charles Gore took a similar view: 'Paul lays very little stress upon the connexion of the earth's present condition with humans, if he even alludes to it. He only says it was subjected to vanity by the decree of the Creator, and that with a glorious prospect.'[22]

Certainly it is the glorious prospect awaiting the whole of creation rather than its present frustrated state that is the overriding theme of this passage. It is not talking about restoring a primitive innocence and harmony that was lost in some past fall but about bringing about the mature fulfilment that was always the Lord's ultimate purpose for his creation. The whole stress is on hope and liberation. These are of course two themes which have much engaged academic theologians in the latter part of the twentieth century, but disappointingly they have tended to concentrate only on the human condition and not to follow Paul in applying hope and liberation to the whole cosmos. We could do with picking up Paul's wider perspective here. We could also do with acknowledging his intense physicality. It is highly significant that he describes the present groanings of creation as resembling the pains and travails of a woman in labour. For him it is indeed new birth that Christ has made possible in the physical as well as in the spiritual sphere. That this new birth and new creation has a physical dimension is made clear by his reference at the end of the passage to the redemption of our bodies. Like the author of Revelation he is looking forward to the creation of a new heaven and a new earth and not just of some disembodied spiritual existence in the afterlife.

It is clear also that Paul sees humans as having an important role to play in bringing about this new creation. He preserves from the Genesis accounts of the fall a sense of man's responsibility for the natural world, but the accent is now wholly positive rather than wholly negative. The human race is not portrayed as the agent responsible for the fall of nature but as the instrument which will lift it up to God and to its fulfilment and destiny. This is why 'the creation waits with eager longing for the revealing of the sons of God.' As the report of a Church of England working party set up in 1974 to look into the whole question of Christian attitudes to nature put it: 'Both men and nature are unfinished, and they move along now not simply under laws of nature, but towards goals which man has a share in setting.'[23]

Underlying Paul's compelling and confident conviction of the ultimate liberation of the whole of creation from its imperfection and frustration is, of course, his belief in the resurrection of Jesus Christ, the One who inaugurated the new creation, who conquered death and decay and in whom all things will be gathered together. This same sense of the cosmic significance of the Messiah can be found in Isaiah's prophetic vision of the wolf dwelling with the kid and the lion eating straw like the ox. It lies behind Irenaeus' view of the destiny to which an immature world is being led and Teilhard de Chardin's image of the Omega point to which all things are moving and on which all things are converging. All see Jesus as the cosmic Christ, the One sent by God to redeem matter as well as man. It is high time that we too began to see him in this light.

4

The cosmic Christ
Who is this that even
the winds and sea obey him?

The Old Testament looks longingly forward to the time when harmony will reign both within the world of nature and between humans and the rest of creation – when the wolf and lamb will dwell together, the lion will eat straw and the little child shall lead them. The New Testament tells us of the one who brings that state of affairs about by inaugurating the new creation, Jesus, he who will be all in all, the cosmic Christ.

Interpreting Jesus in this light requires a major shift of thought for western theology. The eastern Orthodox tradition has always regarded Christ in cosmic terms, as the one who by his life sanctified all matter and through his death and resurrection carries up the whole of creation to God. But in the West our tendency has been to think in purely anthropocentric terms about the Jesus of history, the man who lived in Galilee 2000 years ago, whose actions and message relate only to human beings. If he is seen as saying anything about the rest of creation it is usually to stress the idea of man's dominion. St Augustine, for example, interpreted the Gospel stories of the Gadarene swine and the cursing of the barren fig tree as confirmation that Christians should view nature as a totally profane sphere:

Christ himself shows that to refrain from the killing of animals and the destroying of plants is the height of superstition, for judging that there are no common rights between us and the beasts and trees, he sent the devils into a herd of swine and with a curse withered the tree on which he found no fruit.[1]

74

But is it true that Our Lord had such a negative attitude to the non-human parts of creation? When we think of Jesus as he is portrayed in the Gospels we rightly think of a man who spent much of his time consorting with people – and particularly with the poorest, the most marginal and the most despised – a man who healed and who taught and who preached. But we miss an important dimension of his life and work if we concentrate simply on Jesus' interaction with other human beings. The Gospels also show him as having a unique power of communion with the non-human world, with animals, plants, even with the physical elements of wind and wave.

We are perhaps given an early hint of this communion in St Luke's Gospel where the story of Christ's nativity is set in a manger. In picturing the infant Jesus as lying on a bed of straw surrounded by cows and sheep and oxen children's Christmas story-books may well embody a deep truth about Our Lord's relationship with nature that we tend to overlook in the adult church. Previous generations have been more ready to make the connection that this imagery suggests. In 1655 the diarist Ralph Josselin dreamed that Christ was born in a stable 'because he was the redeemer of man and beast out of their bondage by the Fall'.[2] In the Victorian countryside on Christmas Eve horses and oxen were rumoured to kneel in their stables and even bees were thought to give out a special buzz. This belief is nicely expressed in Thomas Hardy's poem, 'The Oxen':

> Christmas Eve, and twelve of the clock.
>   'Now they are all on their knees',
> An elder said as we sat in a flock
>   By the embers in hearthside ease.
> We pictured the meek mild creatures where
>   They dwelt in their strawy pen,
> Nor did it occur to one of us there
>   To doubt they were kneeling then.

Another early indication of Jesus' special relationship with the animal world is given in St Mark's account of his temptation in the wilderness where we are told that 'he was with the wild beasts' (Mark 1:13). This may seem an unimportant little aside but it presents a striking image that is worthy of some comment. Here is a man thrown into a barren desert among savage animals who is yet left untouched by them. Indeed he is described as being with them as though they are his companions and friends. There are clear echoes of Daniel's experience in the den of lions where he is unharmed because he trusted in God. We are also reminded of Isaiah's prediction of the harmony that will reign in the natural world, and in relations between humans and animals, with the coming of the Messiah. Can it be, indeed, that the wild beasts of the wilderness recognise Jesus as the Son of God sent into the world to perfect creation, to lift up all creatures and gather them in to the everlasting embrace of their loving Father?

It is not just animals who are portrayed in the Gospels as recognising the cosmic Christ in their midst. The miracle story of the stilling of the storm suggests that the inanimate physical elements of wind and wave also respond to Jesus in a unique way:

On that day, when evening had come, he said to them, 'Let us go across to the other side.' And leaving the crowd, they took him with them in the boat, just as he was. And other boats were with him. And a great storm of wind arose, and the waves beat into the boat, so that the boat was already filling. But he was in the stern, asleep on the cushion; and they woke him and said to him, 'Teacher, do you not care if we perish?' And he awoke and rebuked the wind, and said to the sea, 'Peace! Be still!' And the wind ceased, and there was a great calm. He said to them, 'Why are you afraid? Have you no faith?' And they were filled with awe, and said to one another, 'Who then is this, that even wind and sea obey him?' (Mark 4: 35–41).

Like the miracle story that follows it about Jesus walking on the water, the account of his stilling of the storm can be read partly as a response to the theme of *Chaoskampf* which we have already seen was a dominant motif in the Old Testament creation narrative. Jesus is being portrayed by the Gospel writers as the One who can uniquely overcome the forces of chaos that are constantly threatening to disturb the natural world, and in particular as the One who can subdue that most threatening and feared of all the natural elements, the sea. We are taken back to similar instances of God's power recorded in the Psalms: 'he made the storm be still, and the waves of the sea were hushed' (Ps. 107:29). The suggestion is clearly being made that in stilling the storm and walking on the water, Jesus is demonstrating that the Lord's power is present in him on earth as it was in creation. But these miracle stories surely also suggest that Jesus is not interested simply in subduing the forces of nature; he is also trying to evoke a response from them just as he seeks a response from his human disciples. The account of the stilling of the storm speaks very specifically of him addressing the wind and the waves. They reply to him by ceasing their roaring and falling silent. There is a suggestion here of a dialogue and almost of a conversion of the fallen, chaotic natural elements. George Matheson, the blind nineteenth-century Scottish minister and theologian, was struck by this aspect of the story. 'It is the quality of the followers of Jesus that awakes our wonder,' he wrote in a meditation based on this story, 'They are drawn from the winds and the sea – from the sphere of wayward forces.'[3]

By so often trying to explain away the so-called nature miracles and concentrating simply on the ones that involve only human beings, we have considerably diminished the scope of Jesus' activities and concerns. He was not just the man who healed lepers and made the blind to see. He was also the man who stilled the storm and walked on the water, whom the wild beasts did not harm; who chose to enter Jerusalem seated on a colt; who often communed with nature, going up into the hills to pray or walking by the side of the lake. Even the miracles of Jesus that do apparently involve only human beings show an interesting interaction with nature and a recognition of its beneficial effects. In the story recounted in John 9 he is portrayed as restoring the sight of a blind man by enlisting the healing powers of nature, first anointing his eyes with clay and then telling him to wash in the sacred pool of Siloam.

It is surely no coincidence that Jesus chose to put across his message in the form of parables filled with images from the natural world – from mustard seeds and grains of sand to vineyards and fields of wheat. C. H. Dodd has suggested that the use of such images 'arises from a conviction that there is no mere analogy, but an inward affinity between the natural order and the spiritual order; or as we might put it in the language of the parables themselves, the kingdom of God is intrinsically like the processes of nature'.[4]

One of Jesus' favourite techniques was to compare the trusting nature of the animals and birds with the anxieties and fretfulness of man. This is perhaps most beautifully expressed in Matthew 6:26–30:

> Look at the birds of the air; they neither sow nor reap nor gather into barns, and yet your heavenly Father feeds them. Are you not of more value than they? . . . Consider the lillies of the fields, how they grow; they neither toil nor spin; yet I tell you, even Solomon in all his glory was not arrayed like one of these. But if God so clothes the grass of the field, which today is alive and tomorrow is thrown into the oven, will he not much more clothe you, O men of little faith?

It is of course possible to interpret those sayings in two very different ways. Like so much of what Jesus says they have an ambiguity and subtlety that is part of their mysterious and universal power. We have tended to take them as indicating how much more important to God man is than the birds and the flowers. Certainly the passage quoted above underlines the unique value of human life to God. But it also points very clearly to the beauty and splendour of the natural world and its enduring significance to the Creator of all things. Many of Jesus' parables and sayings express this sense of the divineness of the natural order. This is something that is coming to be appreciated much more by New Testament scholars as they look anew at the wisdom sayings and aphorisms recorded in the Gospels and find one of their most significant themes to be God's continuing care and sustaining love for all his creation. Interestingly, Old Testament scholars are also increasingly stressing the importance of a 'static' theology of divine blessing and divine presence rather than of the concepts of redemption and salvation.[5] There is both a universality and a particularity about God's sustaining care as it is portrayed in the Gospels. Jesus reminds his hearers that God 'makes his sun rise on the evil and on the good, and sends rain on the just and the unjust' (Matt. 5:45). He also tells them: 'Are not two sparrows sold for a penny? And not one of them will fall to the ground without your Father's will' (Matt. 10:29).

In death, as in life, Jesus is portrayed in the Gospels as one who is in harmony with nature. At the moment of his death the earth responds by shaking violently and the sun's light is eclipsed. Several of the great English mystics have seen animals suffering alongside the crucified Christ. For Margery Kempe in the sixteenth century the sight of a horse being ill-treated inspired a vision of Jesus being scourged. In the following century William Bowling was gripped by the conviction that 'Christ shed his blood for kine and horses as well as for men'.[6] The most powerful vision of the whole of creation suffering with Christ in his crucifixion was surely that experienced by Dame Julian of Norwich in the revelations that came to her at the end of the fourteenth century:

> Here I saw a great oneing betwixt Christ and us, to mine understanding: for when He was in pain, we were in pain. And all creatures that might suffer pain, suffered with Him: that is to say, all creatures that God hath made to our service. The firmament, the earth, failed for sorrow in their Nature in the time of Christ's dying. For it belongeth naturally to their property to know him for their God, in whom all their virtue standeth: when He failed, then behoved it needs to them, because of kindness between them, to fail with Him, as much as they might, for sorrow of His pains.[7]

There is a strong Christian tradition, not founded explicitly on any statement in the Gospels though strongly suggested in Ephesians 4:8–10 and 1 Peter 3:19 and powerfully attested in our creeds, that for the three days after his death Christ descended into the depths of the earth. In an arresting and powerful phrase, Gerrard Winstanley portrayed the dead Jesus as 'lying in the grave, like a corn of wheat buried under the clods for a time'. He went on to say, 'The body of Christ is where the Father is, in the earth, purifying the earth; and his Spirit is entered into the whole creation, which is the heavenly glory where the Father dwells.'[8]

It is surely significant that the Gospels portray the great dramas of Jesus' crucifixion and resurrection as taking place in the setting of a garden. It is in a garden that he chooses to spend his last moments alone on earth as a free man and where he is seized and arrested. He is crucified near a garden, buried in a garden and makes his first resurrection appearance in a garden where he is actually mistaken for the gardener by Mary Magdalene. The parallels with the Old Testament stories of the creation and the fall are surely not coincidental. In *Only One Way Left* Lord MacLeod of Fuinary has made much of the garden setting that links the biblical accounts of the fall and the resurrection. For him it shows God's intention and purpose for humans as co-operators with him in the work of creation. In the Garden of Eden humans try to run the show themselves and become alienated from both God and nature as a result. Jesus' crucifixion and resurrection in a garden restores the broken relationships:

In the place where Jesus was crucified there was a garden and in the garden a new tomb. From that tomb the New Man rose lifting from its bondage the whole body of things as well as of men. True Nature was re-established. Man in Christ is made the heir once more of a new earth. No wonder Mary, on the Resurrection morning thought he was the gardener for indeed he was – the new Adam and the New Man; the restored co-operation.[9]

The notion of Jesus as the second Adam, the One sent by God not just to perfect humanity but to restore harmony between humans and nature and to lift the whole of creation to God, is also powerfully suggested by the image of the cross as a counterpart of the tree in the middle of the Garden of Eden. There has been a long Christian tradition of seeing the cross on Calvary as standing in the same spot at the centre of the earth as the tree from which Adam and Eve plucked the forbidden fruit. In eastern Orthodoxy in particular, this imagery has been developed to portray the holistic and cosmic significance of the crucified Christ. The cross, made from the wood of the tree of good and evil, is seen as representing the cosmic tree of life. A homily of pseudo-Chrysostom speaks of the cross as a tree 'which rises from the earth to the heavens. A plant immortal, it stands at the centre of heaven and of earth; strong pillar of the universe, bond of all things, support of all the inhabited earth'. The Byzantine liturgy sings of 'the tree of life planted on Calvary, the tree on which the King of ages wrought our salvation . . . springing from the depths of the earth and rising to the centre of the earth, sanctifying the Universe unto its limits'.[10]

In talking about the second Adam who redeems and gathers up the entire created order we have moved from a consideration of the historical Jesus to the more difficult but no less important realms of Christology and soteriology – the questions of who Jesus was and the nature and significance of his saving work. In these fields just as in the study of the historical figure whose life is described in the Gospels our besetting sin of anthropocentrism had given us a very narrow perspective. Conventional Christology in the West at least tends to portray Jesus as the Son of God sent to redeem mankind by dying for our sins and to open the way to eternal life for us by rising from the dead. His role is often put in very individual terms, with virtually no acknowledgement that it might have a universal significance for all humanity, let alone for the rest of creation.

Yet this is not how the New Testament speaks of the nature and scope of Jesus' saving work. One of the most vivid Christological titles which is applied to Jesus in the Gospels is drawn directly from the animal world and stresses the cosmic scope of his redemptive sweep. It is put into the mouth of

John the Baptist in the first chapter of the Fourth Gospel: 'Behold, the Lamb of God, who takes away the sin of the world!' Traditionally this has been seen as a reference either to the Passover lamb or to the sacrificial lambs in Hebrew worship. Modern New Testament scholarship has cast some doubt on whether it was, in fact, one or both of these images that the author of the Fourth Gospel had in mind when he produced this statement. But what is beyond doubt is that he intended to compare Jesus to those vulnerable and innocent creatures that we see gambolling in the fields in spring and suckling so intently at their mothers' breasts. He also clearly intended to proclaim that it is the sins of the world which Christ takes away, not just the sins of humankind.

In the Book of Revelation the image of Christ as the Lamb of God is, of course, picked up and used again and again. In at least one passage the Lamb becomes the focus of that kind of recognition and worship by all God's creatures that we have already seen being prophesied in the Psalms: 'And I heard every creature in heaven and on earth and under the earth and in the sea, and all therein, saying, "To him who sits upon the throne and to the Lamb be blessing and honour and glory and might for ever and ever!" ' (Rev. 5:13).

A closer look at other passages in the New Testament where reference is made to the nature of Christ's saving work reveals a similar note of cosmic universality. Although one would hardly guess it from most creeds and confessions with their talk of 'us men and our salvation', the two best-known statements of the purpose of Christ's mission both see the cosmos (the Greek word that is actually used) rather than mankind as the object of salvation: 'For God so loved the world that he gave his only Son' (John 3:16); and 'in Christ God was reconciling the world to himself' (2 Cor. 5:19). The notion of Christ as a universal and cosmic saviour is also conveyed by the use of the Greek phrase τα παντα (all things) in the other great Christological statements of St Paul in his epistles to the early Christian communities. In Ephesians 1:10 he talks of God's plan in Christ 'to unite all things in him, things in heaven and things on earth'. In Hebrews 1:2 he talks of God speaking through his Son, 'whom he appointed the heir of all things'. In Colossians 1:16–20, Christ's role both as Creator and perfecter are given a clearly cosmic dimension:

> in him all things were created, in heaven and on earth, visible and invisible . . . all things were created through him and for him. He is before all things and in him all things hold together . . . For in him all the fullness of God was pleased to dwell, and through him to reconcile all things, whether on earth or heaven, making peace by the blood of his cross.

Paul's words remind us of Jesus' central role in the creation of the world. In classical Christian doctrine he is, of course, regarded as the agent of creation, the Word through whom, in the well-known words of the prologue to St John's Gospel, all things were made and without whom was not anything made that was made. In our modern concentration on Jesus as saviour and redeemer we have tended to forget his role as Creator. We have also lost that sense which Paul conveys so clearly of Jesus Christ as the one in whom all things hold together and are reconciled. The Greek verb which Paul uses, ἀνακεφαλαιοω, is usually translated as gathering together in one. This notion of Christ as the perfecter and unifier of the disjointed cosmos fits well with the approach explored in the previous chapter which interprets the doctrine of the fall as pointing to the world's immaturity and incompleteness. It has been given powerful pictorial expression in Salvador Dali's well-known painting 'Christ of St John of the Cross' which hangs in Glasgow Art Gallery. The artist was inspired by a 'cosmic dream' in which he saw an image representing 'th nucleus of the atom – the very unity of the Universe – C'

The idea that Jesus was sent by God to perfect ʳ up all creation was much stressed by maɲ Church Fathers. St Irenaeus taught that Son into the world he was recapitula within a new divine organism. H that God is constantly active wiʇ continuously creating new life and su is. But with the Incarnation these processes were gathered up and concentrated in a unique way. God entered the world so that it could be carried up to him and the whole of creation could participate in his glory. As Irenaeus put it, 'By the word of God everything is under the economy of redemption. The Son of God was crucified for all and for everything, having traced the sign of the Cross on all things.'[11]

Jesus Christ, fully physical and fully divine, is the link that binds the creation of the world with its final consummation just as he is the link between the material and spiritual. One of the key links in that chain is the cross, the wooden tree on which God expressed his total identification and solidarity with suffering nature. Another is the resurrection, understood as a physical as well as a spiritual event, as George Hendry reminds us:

> Christians who believe in the resurrection cannot restrict their hope to a future life for themselves; they extend it to the whole created world, which, as it proceeded from God in its entirety at the beginning, will, through his faithfulness, attested in resurrection, proceed towards him in its entirety at the end. The word that was in the beginning, and through whom all things were made, will receive its appropriate response from all things – 'and earth repeat the long Amen'.[12]

We badly need in the West to recover a sense of Jesus as the one in whom all things hold together, to rediscover the cosmic dimension of Christ that has been lost in centuries of anthropocentric thinking about purely human salvation. Among our best guides back into those long abandoned ways of thinking are those in our own western tradition, Catholic and Protestant, who have found Christ in the very elements of nature. The seventeenth-century Spanish mystic St John of the Cross described Jesus in his 'Song of the Bride' as 'the mountains, he lonely wooden valleys, the strange islands, the noisy ers, the whistling wind in love'.[13] Gerrard Winstanley, his lish Puritan contemporary, observed that: 'the great , wherein are varieties of creatures, Sun, Moon, Stars,

Earth, Grass, Plants, Cattle, Fish, Fowl and Man, all sweetly conjoined to preserve each other, is no other but Christ spread forth in the Creation'.[14] In our own century Pierre Teilhard de Chardin talks of Jesus as 'the hidden power stirring in the heart of all nature' while the contemporary process theologian John Cobb sees Christ as the creative, transforming principle lurking in all matter, animate and inanimate.[15]

Such statements are often objected to on the grounds that they come close to pantheism, deifying nature and suggesting that God is simply the sum total of everything that exists. In fact they are more correctly identified as panentheistic, expressing the notion that God includes the world and yet exceeds it, that everything is in him and he is in everything while still having an independent identity. Something close to this idea is surely what Paul is getting at in the passages quoted above and even more in his confident assertion that Christ is 'all, and in all' (Col. 3:11) and his majestic statement about the end time when Christ has completed his work of reconciling and gathering up all creation 'that God may be all in all' (1 Cor. 15:28 AV). A panentheistic view of God is surely also wholly consonant with two of the most important features of Christian faith and worship – the doctrine of the Incarnation and the celebration of sacraments. If it means anything at all, Incarnation must surely point to God's presence through Christ in the physical world – he does not just exist outside it and look on from the heavens. By believing in the efficacy of sacraments, the things of earth lifted up to heaven, Christians are proclaiming both the presence of God through Christ in the physical elements and also the sacred nature of matter, whose destiny it is to be carried up to the Creator.

The eastern Orthodox churches have always adopted a highly sacramental approach towards nature which we in the West would do well to follow if we want to make Christianity environment-friendly once again. It is beautifully expressed by Professor Paul Evdokinov:

The destiny of the element of water is to participate in the mystery of the Epiphany; the destiny of the earth is to

receive the body of the Lord for the repose of the Great
Saturday; and the destiny of stone is to end as the sealed
tomb and as the stone rolled away before the myrrh-bearing
women. Olive oil and water find their fulfilment as conduc-
tors of grace to regenerated man; the wheat and the vine
culminate in the Eucharistic cup. Everything refers to the
Incarnation and everything leads to the Lord.[16]

pomegranets too

The writings of Teilhard de Chardin show a similar sacramental approach to nature. As we have already seen, for
him matter was indeed the divine milieu: 'The universe is
physically impregnated to the very core of its matter by the
influence of Christ's super-human nature.'[17] Building on his
strong incarnational theology, his Catholic sacramentalism
and his work as a biologist, he developed a remarkable sense
of Christ's continuous and dynamic presence in the world:

All round us Christ is physically active in order to control
all things. From the ultimate vibration of the atom to the
loftiest mystical contemplation; from the lightest breeze
that ruffles the air to the broadest currents of life and
thought, he ceaselessly animates, without disturbing, all
the earth's processes. And in return Christ gains physically
from every one of them. Everything that is good in the
Universe is gathered up by the Incarnate Word.[18]

Perhaps more than any other modern theologian, Teilhard
is the supreme exponent of the idea of the cosmic Christ. His
writings reach back to the Christological statements of St
Paul and recall the recapitulatory language of Irenaeus and
the early Fathers. They also point forward to much contemporary process theology. Not the least of the services that he
has performed for the cause of Green Christianity is to point
out very clearly how the universality of Christ's saving role
can only be maintained if the doctrine of the fall is taken
seriously and also seen in universal terms:

Redemption is immediately seen to be universal because it
provides the remedy for a state of things – the presence

everywhere of disorder – which is bound up in the most elemental condition of the universe in the process of creation . . . In order for Christ to be universal it is necessary that redemption and therefore the fall be extended to the whole of the universe . . . To safeguard the Christian view of Christ the Redeemer, it is clearly necessary that we keep original sin as large as the world, otherwise Christ will have saved only part of the world and not be the Centre of everything.[19]

If Christians are to have a positive and constructive dialogue with the growing Green movement and with all who are concerned about the future of our planet, we need to speak in this wide language about the cosmic Christ. We need to proclaim that in becoming incarnate through Jesus God showed his desire to perfect and to draw up into himself not just human beings but the whole of his wonderful creation. We need to develop a view of physical matter as something that is sacred rather than profane, a view which rests on the sacraments that our Lord himself instituted and commanded us to continue as a perpetual memorial of his passion and death. We are not without guides as we embark on this way of thinking about our faith. I have already mentioned the extent to which we can learn from the eastern Orthodox churches which have always held to the notion of the deification of the entire cosmos rather than the narrower idea of personal human salvation. Two brief extracts from the writings of leading Orthodox theologians of the present century beautifully express this tradition of worshipping Christ in cosmic terms as the redeemer of all creation:

Not only human nature but the whole universe and the whole of cosmic life was transformed after the coming of Christ. When the Blood of Christ shed upon Calvary touched the earth, earth became a new thing, and it is only the limitation of our receptive faculties which prevent us from seeing it with our very eyes.[20]

Christ walked this earth: He admired its flowers and in his
parables He spoke of the things of this world as figures of
the heavens; He was baptized in the waters of the Jordan,
He spent the three days in the bosom of the earth; there is
nothing in this world which has remained a stranger to His
humanity and has not received the imprint of the Holy
Spirit.[21]

There is also a rich body of material in our western Christian tradition which can help us recapture our lost sense of
the cosmic Christ. Some of it I have quoted in this chapter.
Another valuable source is verses from long-neglected and
forgotten hymns. How many congregations today sing that
fine hymn by the nineteenth-century Church of Scotland minister John Ross Macduff, which begins 'Christ is coming! Let
creation from her groans and travails cease', the only hymn
I know to be based on that great passage on the theology of
nature in Romans 8:18–25. Another hymn which describes
Christ's redemptive work in the world of nature is tucked
away in the stewardship and service section of the current
edition of the *Church Hymnary*, and as far as I know is not
found in any other modern hymn book. Written in 1900 by
a Dorset vicar, George Clement Martin, it picks up several
of the themes dwelt on in this book:

Almighty Father of all things that be,
Our life, our work, we consecrate to thee,
Whose heavens declare thy glory from above,
Whose earth below is witness to thy love.

For well we know this weary, soiled earth
Is yet Thine own by right of its new birth,
Since that great Cross upreared on Calvary
Redeemed it from its fault and shame to thee.

Thine still the changeful beauty of the hills,
The purple valleys flecked with silver rills,
The ocean glistening 'neath the golden rays;
They all are thine, and voiceless speak thy praise.

The nineteenth-century Congregational minister Thomas Lynch wrote a striking hymn based on the miracle of walking on the water. I have only been able to find it in the 1933 edition of the *Baptist Hymn Book* but it is surely worth resurrecting, if only for these lines:

> O where is he that trod the sea?
>   Oh where is he that spake –
> And dark waves, rolling heavily,
>   A grassy smoothness take?

Perhaps the hymn that speaks most strikingly and effectively of the cosmic Christ is the original version of one of our most popular carols, 'Hark! the herald angels sing'. When Charles Wesley wrote it in 1739 it had a different title, 'Hark how all the welkin rings' and included two verses which were dropped when the hymn was given its modern form in 1755. They deserve immediate reinstatement in the urgent battle to make Christianity Green once again:

> Joyful, all ye nations rise,
>   Join the triumph of the skies;
> Universal nature say:
>   'Christ the Lord is born today'.

> Now display thy saving power,
>   Ruined nature now restore,
> Now in mystic union join
>   Thine to ours and ours to thine.

5

The role of human beings
*Thou hast given him dominion
over the works of thy hands*

Does Christianity offer a distinctive insight into the proper
relationship between human beings and the rest of creation?
Do Christians indeed have a special contribution to make to
the Green movement and the battle to preserve the natural
environment from the many threats that are now facing it?
Of course, as part of the human race, we can all do our bit
by consuming less energy, going in for organic gardening,
recycling our waste paper, bottles and cans and using ozone-
friendly aerosols. But is there something more that we can
do because of our faith?

The Bible portrays humans as occupying a unique place
and fulfilling a key role in the working out of God's plan for
the whole of his creation. Alone among all his creatures,
humans are fashioned by God in his own image. They are
also given a clear commission by him to exercise dominion
over the rest of creation. As we have seen, this is far from
being the warrant for domination and exploitation that it has
so often been taken to be. Rather it suggests that there is a
special role and responsibility for humans *vis-á-vis* the rest of
creation. Psalm 8 asks God the question 'What is man that
thou art mindful of him?' and gives its own answer: 'Thou
hast given him dominion over the works of thy hands'. Paul
talks in Romans 8:19 about the whole of creation waiting
'with eager longing for the revealing of the sons of God'.

What exactly is the role that we are called as human beings
to exercise? It is certainly not just standing back and letting
wild nature rule. We may have gone far too far in the West
in objectifying and taming nature but the whole Christian
tradition is clear that man is not there simply to worship wild

nature. We stand together with nature as fellow-sufferers in this world of pain and sorrow and we also stand together with God as co-operators in his plan to perfect and complete creation. As we have already observed, Christianity is not compatible with an outlook which regards humanity as a wholly negative and destructive species and which draws its spiritual strength from the pagan worship of wild nature. The kind of sentiments expressed in Wilfred Scawen Blunt's poem, 'Satan Absolved' which portrays God preferring virgin nature before man, 'that lewd bare-buttocked ape', arrived on the scene have no part in the Christian approach to nature. The Bible does not talk of a perfect world of nature which is violated by man. Rather it portrays everything as being imperfect and engaged in a continuous process of completion and fulfilment. In that process humans are given a central role.

The principle of stewardship has long been prominent in Christian thought about the relationship of humans to their environment. It was classically stated in the seventeenth century by Sir Matthew Hale:

The end of man's creation was that he should be the viceroy of the great God of heaven and earth in this inferior world; his steward, bailiff or farmer of this goodly farm of the lower world. Only for this reason was man invested with power, authority, right, dominion, trust and care, to correct and abridge the excesses and cruelties of the fiercer animals, to give protection and defence to the mansuete (tame) and useful, to preserve the species of divers vegetables, to improve them and others, to correct the redundance of unprofitable vegetables, to preserve the face of the earth in beauty, usefulness and fruitfulness.[1]

This notion of stewardship takes up the biblical theme of dominion in a way that respects God's sovereignty over all the earth. A good steward acts as a faithful deputy of God sustaining his creation and preserving it for future generations. David Hartley, the eighteenth-century philosopher, wrote of the relationship between humans and animals: 'We seem to be in the place of God to them and we are obliged by the same tenure to be their guardians and benefactors.'[2] Stewardship involves accountability – we are answerable to God for the way we manage his world during our time here. It also suggests an active and creative role in respect of the earth which we have been given responsibility for. We are to be gardeners as well as guardians.

Indeed there is much to be said for the idea that we are gardeners of creation. For a start it is of course profoundly biblical. In the earlier Yahwehist account of creation Adam is set in the Garden of Eden to till and keep it. Lord MacLeod of Fuinary has argued that this provides us with a model for the proper relationship between man and the natural world.

> He starts off as God's co-operator in a garden where everything is lovely. It is important that it is a garden. True nature, for the Bible, is not what we generally picture it: Virgin Soil before man has had a hand in it. The work of man in tillage is as essential as the rain for bringing into existence true nature. God the eternal worker created man to be a worker. The purpose of creation is fulfilled when worker meets worker in the fruit of their co-operation. Thus, further, as the type of true nature is not vegetation but a garden, so the expression of spiritual fulfilment is not 'the natural' (in modern thinking), nor even the cultivated wheat and vine, but Bread and Wine, products of Divine-human co-operation.[3]

The idea that humans have been placed on earth by God primarily as gardeners to cultivate it has appealed to Christians of widely different persuasions. In the sixth century St Benedict, founder of western monasticism, saw husbandry as a way of providing a sustainable lifestyle for his monks which fitted in with the rhythm of the seasons and provided a physical counterpart to their spiritual labours of prayer and contemplation. Gardening has continued to be a mainstay of monastic communities ever since. The seventh-century Greek theologian St Maximus wrote that the purpose of human life was to establish harmony between the masculine and femi-

92

nine, cultivate the earth into Paradise, reunite the earth and heaven and finally restore to God the universe thus ordered according to his divine plan. In seventeenth-century England this view of humans as divinely appointed gardeners of creation was held by several notable figures. Edward Hyde, Earl of Clarendon, felt that God had 'committed the earth to man to be by him cultivated and polished'.[4] The mystic Roger Crab gave a new twist to the popular belief that we are closer to God in a garden: 'When I was in my earthly garden a-digging with my spade I saw forth into the Paradise of God from whence my father Adam was cast forth.'[5] Gerrard Winstanley was more down to earth, and more organic. 'True religion and undefiled', he observed, 'is to let everyone quietly have earth to manure.'[6]

In our own time gardening has been given further theological blessing by the ecologically-minded American Passionist priest Thomas Berry:

> Gardening is an active participation in the deepest mysteries of the universe. By gardening our children learn that they constitute with all growing things a single community of life. They learn to nurture and be nurtured in a universe that is always precarious but ultimately benign. They learn profound reasons for the seasonal rituals of the great religious traditions.[7]

Gardening is, of course, an activity largely carried out for man's own benefit. It is possible to find other models of good stewardship which are rather less anthropocentric. If Adam is the founding father of gardening, Noah surely fulfils that role for wildlife conservation. His action in taking into the ark a breeding pair of every living species represents stewardship of a less anthropocentric sort. But is even this kind of stewardship enough? Does it really measure up to our high calling and our unique creation in the image of God? I find myself in agreement with Paulos Gregorios when he writes in *The Human Presence*:

Replacing the concept of domination with the concept of

stewardship will not lead us very far, for even in the latter there lies the hidden possibility of the objectification and alienation which are the root causes of the sickness of our civilisation . . . We would still reducing nature to 'nothing but', that is, nothing but an object given into our hands for safe keeping and good management.[8]

Jesus, after all, was more than a steward of the natural world. He loved it and communed with it to such an extent that it responded by allowing him to walk on the water, still the storm and wander with the wild beasts in the wilderness without being harmed. There may be no actual references in the Gospels to specific acts of kindness to animals but the Bible as a whole carries this message. The Book of Proverbs contains the advice that 'a righteous man has regard for the life of his beast' (Prov. 12:10). Many of the early Church Fathers adopted an attitude of love and kindness to animals which was informed by their sense of Christ's cosmic purpose and the sanctity of all creation. In answer to the question 'what is a charitable heart' Isaac Syrus, the seventh-century bishop of Nineveh, affirmed 'it is a heart which is burning with charity for the whole of creation, for men, for the birds, for the beasts, for the demons – for all creatures'.[9]

The lives of the great Celtic saints who first brought the Christian Gospel to our land show a similar reverence for and communion with nature that went far beyond mere stewardship. Often they achieved remarkable relationships with animals and birds. Kevin of Glendalough was an Irish saint who died early in the seventh century. The story goes that one Lent while he was engaged in his thirty-day vigil in a wattled pen with a flagstone as his bed, a blackbird came and built its nest on his outstretched palm and hatched her brood there. Kevin also provides what must surely be one of the earliest ever recorded examples of resistance to developers' plans on the grounds that they would destroy the countryside. His reaction to a proposal to build a monastery on the Wicklow Hills should surely make him the patron saint of conservationists everywhere: 'I have no wish that the creatures of God should be moved because of me. My God can help that place in some other fashion. And moreover, all the wild creatures on these mountains are my housemates, gentle and familiar with me, and they would be sad at this.'[10]

Adamnan's celebrated Life of St Columba shows a man totally in communion with the natural world around him, captivated by the waves that broke on the strand of Iona, praying that he might see the sea monsters, 'the greatest of all wonders', and calming a storm when he and his companions were suddenly endangered in a boat. It also contains this lovely story which shows that he regarded the birds who visited his island as being just as important as the human pilgrims:

At one time, when the Saint was living in the island of Io, he called in one of the brothers, and thus addressed him: 'On the third day from this that dawns, you must watch in the western part of this island, sitting above the sea-shore: for after the ninth hour of the day a guest will arrive from the northern region of Ireland, very tired and weary, a crane that has been tossed by winds through long circuits of the air. And with its strength almost exhausted it will fall near you and lie upon the shore. You will take heed to lift it tenderly, and carry it to the house near by; and, having taken it in as a guest for three days and nights, you will wait upon it and feed it with anxious care. And afterwards, at the end of the three days, revived and not wishing to be longer in pilgrimage with us, it will return with fully recovered strength to the sweet district in Ireland from which at first it came. I commend it to you thus earnestly, for this reason, that it comes from the district of our fathers.'

The brother obeyed; and on the third day, after the ninth hour, as he had been bidden, he awaited the coming of the foreknown guest. When it arrived, he lifted it from the shore where it had fallen; in its weakness, he carried it to the lodging; in its hunger, he fed it. When he returned to the monastery in the evening, the Saint, not questioning but affirming said to him: 'God bless you, my son, because you have tended well the pilgrim guest.'[11]

Perhaps the outstanding example of the Christian saint whose faith and life involved a loving communion with the natural world is Francis of Assisi, declared by the Pope in 1980 the patron saint of ecology. There is a danger in over-romanticising this aspect of his life. Francis spent considerably more time surrounded by lepers and down-and-outs than by birds and squirrels. But there is no doubt that he achieved a remarkable communion with such creatures and that his fellow-feeling with them was an integral part of his spirituality, as evidenced in his 'Canticle of the Creatures' quoted on page 41. If St Benedict stands for the principles of stewardship and husbandry, St Francis stands for fellowship with the rest of creation. Stories abound of his kindly treatment of animals, birds and fishes and of their response to him:

> On a lake he was offered a large live fish which he addressed as brother in his usual way and put it back into the water by the boat. The fish played about in the water in front of the man of God; and as if it were attracted by his love, it would not go away from the ship until it received from him his permission with a blessing.[12]

Nor has it been only Celtic and medieval saints who have had a strong sense of man's oneness with the animal kingdom. A hundred years ago the blind Church of Scotland minister George Matheson pondered on the meaning of the Lord's command to humans to have dominion over the fish of the sea and the beasts of the earth and the fowl of the air:

> God never gives dominion to any creature which has not received his image. His image is love. Other things belong to God; but God is love. No creature that has not love will be allowed to have a permanent empire. The father of mercy will not put the reins of government into a hand that has no heart. Dominion is a very solemn thing; it may oppress, crush, destroy. The Father must have a guarantee for its gentleness. What guarantee can there be but His own image – the possession of a nature tender as the Divine? Ye who torture the beast of the field, have you considered the

ground of your authority? Have you pondered why it is that God has given you the dominion? It is because He meant to give you His image ere you began to reign.

My Father, fill me with love for things beneath me. Forbid that I should be cruel to the beasts of the field. Give me the tenderness that is born of reverence. Teach me to revere the creation under me. Was not its life a stream from Thy life? Is not its life a mystery to me even now?

Give me fellowship with beast and bird. Let me enter into sympathy with their hunger, their thirst, their weariness, their cold, their frequent homelessness. Let me give their wants a place in my prayers. Let me remember them in the struggles of the forest. Let me remember them in the neglect of the city. Let me remember them in the winter's frost and snow. Let me be to them what Thou hast been to me – a protector, a Providence.[13]

When Jesus told his disciples, 'In as much as ye did it to one of the least of your brethren ye did it to me,' was he perhaps indicating that we should feed the dumb animals as well as the starving in the Third World and pray for endangered species of plant and insect as well as for homeless and suffering humanity? This is certainly how his words have been interpreted in the eastern Orthodox tradition. Vladimir Solovyev, the nineteenth-century Russian theologian and spiritual writer, held the view that love is the quality that should characterise not only inter-personal relations but also our relation to the cosmic environment. According to Paulos Gregorios, Solovyev believed that:

> our love creates spiritual energies which inwardly transform the cosmos itself, imprinting upon it the image of God as love. The cosmos itself is a living organism within which the pleroma of humanity as an organ has a central and key function almost like the heart or the brain in the body.[14]

St Francis expressed the same sentiment in a rather simpler way when he called all creatures his sisters and brothers.

St Francis has more to tell us than just to be kind to

animals. He also shows us how we can find God through
them. His biographer Bonaventura notes that he began his
spiritual quest with a contemplation of the world and all its
fullness and that it was his wonder at the splendour of creation
that directed him to God. In his own treatise, *The Soul's Journey
to God*, Bonaventura begins with a similar contemplation of
the world and all the creatures within it: 'Whoever is not
enlightened by such splendour of created things is blind,' he
writes, 'for every creature is by its nature a kind of effigy and
likeness of the eternal wisdom.'[15] Many of the great mystics
have shared the same experience, beginning their spiritual
journey by seeing God in the mirror of his creation and being
led on to rise higher in contemplation.

Much the same point is made in Mrs C. F. Alexander's simple
and familiar children's hymn 'All things bright and beautiful'
which lists the wonders of nature, from the little flowers that
open to the purple-headed mountain, and then reminds us:

> He gave us eyes to see them,
> And lips that we might tell
> How great is God Almighty,
> Who has made all things well.

It is all too easy to sentimentalise nature and to think only
of bunches of flowers and birds singing in the trees while
forgetting the suffering, the sacrifice and the conflict that
makes nature red in tooth and claw as well as lush and green.
But it is also easy to ignore the message of nature and fail to
let it lead us to God. Herman Hesse pointed to both these
dangers in a remarkable passage in his novel, *Peter Camenzind*:

> Plenty of people say they 'love nature'. They mean that
> sometimes they are not averse to allowing its proffered
> charms to delight them. They go out and enjoy the beauty
> of the earth, trample down the meadows and gather bun-
> ches of flowers, sprays of foliage, only to throw them down
> or see them wilt at home. That is how they love nature.
> They remember their love on Sundays when the weather is
> fine and they are then carried away by their own sentiment.

And this is generous of them for is not 'Man the crowning glory of Nature'? Alas, yes, 'the crown!'

And so more enthusiastically than ever I explored the basic things of life. I heard the wind sighing in the tree-tops, mountain torrents roaring down the gorges and quiet streams purling across the plains, and I knew that God was speaking in these sounds and that to gain an under-standing of that mysterious tongue with its primitive beauty would be to regain Paradise. There was little of it in books; the Bible alone contains the wonderful expression of the 'groaning and travailing of creation'. Yet I knew deep down inside me that at all times men, similarly overcome by things beyond their comprehension, had abandoned their daily work and gone forth in search of tranquillity so to listen to the hum of creation, contemplate the movements of the clouds, and anchorites, penitents and saints alike, filled with restless longing, stretch out their arms towards the eternal.[16]

How often do we use our eyes to marvel at God's works or pause to listen to the hum of creation? We seem curiously reluctant, almost frightened, to let our souls be moved by the beauties of nature and soar to God through a contemplation of what he has wrought. Yet his works have surely just as much power to lead us to him as his words. 'There are two books from whence I collect my divinity,' noted the seventeenth-century physician Sir Thomas Browne, 'beside that written one of God, another of his servant Nature, that universal and public manuscript, that lies expans'd unto the eyes of all; those that never saw him in the one, have dis-covered him in the other.' Browne went on to commend the so-called heathens for 'knowing better how to join and read these mystical letters than we Christians, who cast a more careless eye on these common hieroglyphics and disdain to suck divinity from the flowers of nature'.[17] The eighteenth-century poet Edward Young put it even more succinctly in his 'Night Thoughts':

Read Nature; Nature is a friend to truth;
Nature is Christian; preaches to mankind;
And bids dead matter aid us in our creed.

It is perhaps time that we revived the traditional discipline
of natural theology, not so much in its old form of finding
proofs for God's existence in the order and design of the
universe but in an appreciation that he can be found in and
through nature. With this awareness, Christians should surely
be encouraging the pursuit of scientific study and natural
history. Science, and particularly biology, has got something
of a dirty name in the late twentieth century – it is associated
with genetic engineering, food technology and other practices
which seem to be manipulative and exploitative of nature and
to be wholly commercial in their purpose. Of course scientists
can be dismissive of the natural world, displaying those callous attitudes that Ralph Waldo Emerson describes so well
in his poem 'Blight':

But these young scholars, who invade our hills,
Bold as the engineer who fells the wood,
And travelling often in the cut he makes,
Love not the flower they pluck, and know it not,
And all their botany is Latin names.

But science can also be approached in a spirit of reverence
and wonder at the beauty and intricacy of God's creation. It
was in such a spirit that the great line of naturalist parsons,
led by the redoubtable Gilbert White of Selborne, combed
the countryside with their notebooks and pocket lenses and
that the Abbé Mendel established the principles of heredity
and genetic selection with peas grown in his monastery
garden. It is important that Christians do not set themselves
resolutely against any kind of scientific study and experiment.
As we have seen, it is from the ranks of scientists that a new
kind of natural theology is emerging, based on a deep respect
for nature and a sense of awe at the complexity and beauty
of creation. After centuries of believing arrogantly that man

knows best we are at last coming to appreciate that there is much that we can learn from nature. This was the message of Jesus Christ in many of his parables and sayings where he contrasted the simple trust and carefree lives of animals and plants with human fretfulness and anxiety.

If Christianity encourages the pursuit of science and natural history, it surely also invites people to become poets and artists of creation. Just over a hundred years ago Matthew Arnold prophesied that poetry would usurp the functions of religion 'to interpret life . . . console . . . and sustain mankind'. Sadly only half his prediction has come true. Although religion has steadily diminished its hold on society and the collective imagination, it is the meretricious banality of the mass media rather than the sweet voice of poetry that has largely taken its place. Perhaps religion and poetry in fact go together and the one cannot flourish without the other. Certainly it is true that much of the most powerful religious writing now is in the form of poetry rather than prose. Significantly when the World Council of Churches working party on justice, peace and the integrity of creation recently addressed the question of the most appropriate role for humans with respect to the rest of creation, they came up with the models of steward, priest and poet. The reason for this last choice was that 'the poet – in the Psalms, Proverbs, Lamentations and the Qoheleth – depicts creation with its myriad forms of life sometimes as accursed and full of melancholy, and other times characterised by joy, exuberance and praise'.[18]

As artists and poets, humans can express and affirm the value of God's non-human creation in a number of different ways. They can represent and distil its beauty and wonder, producing images which touch our imagination and lead us to God. They can also act as co-creators with God, fashioning order out of chaos – one thinks of the sculptor making a work of art out of a rough block of stone that was the product of the violence of earthquake or volcano. Perhaps art does have the power literally to change the world. Certainly that was what C. H. Dodd seemed to be suggesting in his commentary on St Paul's words about creation waiting with eager longing for the revealing of the sons of God: 'If we could all become artists over the whole of life, using our whole environment to express the highest spiritual relations within our reach, is it not possible that the influence of humanity upon the world might change its whole aspect?'[19]

Uniquely among all creatures humans are endowed with the power of speech and the creative gifts of writing, painting and making music. Could it be that we have a responsibility to voice the prayers and express the thanksgivings not just of ourselves but of the whole of creation – that our role is to be not just the mouthpiece of our fellow creatures but perhaps also the channel through which they will find God. This idea is beautifully expressed in a poem written in the early years of this century and addressed 'To Everyman':

> All things search until they find
> God through the gateway of thy mind;
> Highest star and humblest clod
> Turn home through thee to God.
> When thou rejoicest in the rose
> Blissful from earth to heaven she goes;
> Upon thy bosom summer seas
> Escape from their captivities;
> Within thy sleep the sightless eyes
> Of night revisage Paradise;
> In thy soft awe yon mountain high
> To his creator draweth nigh;
> This lonely tarn, reflecting thee,
> Returneth to eternity;
> And thus in thee the circuit vast
> Is rounded and complete at last,
> And, at last, through thee revealed
> To God, what time and space concealed.[20]

Those lines bring together two themes that have figured prominently in this book: the idea of creation as an open, uncompleted process which is moving towards God and the notion of nature groaning in travail, frustrated and unable to voice the praise that it desires to express to its Lord. We are reminded of all those Old Testament references to the hills skipping like lambs and the trees of the field clapping their hands. We are also reminded of the marvellous reciprocity whereby we can find God through nature and nature can find God through us. Here at last we find a role for humans that is consonant with the concept of dominion and fits our unique status as beings created in the image of God and our unique ability to communicate with him but which makes us as much the servants of nature as its masters. We are charged with the awesome responsibility of carrying the rest of creation up to God. We are, indeed, the world's high priests, as George Herbert put it in one of his profoundest poems, 'Providence II':

Of all creatures both in sea and land
Only to man thou hast made known thy ways,
And put the pen alone into his hand,
And made him secretary of thy praise.

Beasts fain would sing; birds ditty to their notes;
Trees would be tuning on their native lute
To thy renown: but all their hands and throats
Are brought to Man, while they are lame and mute.

Man is the world's High Priest: he doth present
The sacrifice for all: while they below
Unto thy service mutter an assent,
Such as springs use that fall, and winds that blow.

The idea that humans are meant to act as the priests of creation has a long pedigree. It goes back at least as far as the early Church Fathers who argued that the role of man is to be the intermediary between the material and the spiritual and to lift up the physical world to God. This profoundly sacramental view of the human task continues to be a feature of the Orthodox outlook today. It is powerfully expressed by the contemporary French Orthodox theologian, Olivier Clement:

If the spiritual destiny of man is inseparable from that of humanity as a whole, it is also inseparable from that of the terrestrial cosmos . . . Man is the personality of the cosmos, its conscious and personal self-expression; it is he who gives meaning to things and who transfigures them. For the universe, man is its hope to receive grace and to be united with God: Man is also the possibility of failure and loss for the universe. Let us recall the fundamental text of St Paul in Romans 8:22. Subject to disorder and death by our fall, the creation waits with eager longing for man's becoming Son of God by grace, which would mean liberation and glory for it also. We are responsible for the world, to the very smallest twigs and plants. We are the word, the 'logos' by which the world expresses itself, by which the world speaks to God; it depends on us whether it blasphemes or it prays, whether it becomes an illusion or wisdom, black magic or celebration. Only through us can the cosmos, as the prolongation of our bodies, have access to eternity.[21]

This kind of perspective has been shared by several theologians outside the Orthodox tradition. In his great Mass over the World celebrated in the desert of China in 1923 Teilhard de Chardin offered the whole cosmos to God and expressed his deep conviction that the destiny of nature is not to be dominated or utilised by man but rather to be offered by him to God. A number of leading Anglicans have recently spoken in similar terms about the role of human beings *vis-à-vis* the rest of creation. For Arthur Peacocke:

Man's role may be conceived as that of priest of creation, as a result of whose activity, the sacrament of creation is reverenced; and who, because he alone is conscious of God, himself and nature, can mediate between insentient nature and God – for a priest is characterised by activity directed towards God on behalf of others.[22]

Hugh Montefiore stresses the creative and redemptive task of humans: 'Man acts not only as co-creator with God in nature but also as co-redeemer in the sense that he assists the purposes of God in the natural world.'[23] Don Cupitt anchors the positive role which humans are called to play in the world in the doctrine of Incarnation: 'The Gospel says that man is not a blight on nature, but crowns her; that God is not the God of the past, but of the future, and that through the incarnation of God in man redemption avails for man himself, and through man's God-inspired work, for nature.'[24]

There are clearly all sorts of ways in which this priestly work can be done, from conservation and animal welfare projects to talking to plants and organic gardening. What it means above all is approaching the rest of creation in a spirit of reverence and seeing nature in sacramental terms because God is there and Christ has been there. It is, of course, in the Eucharist that this sacramental approach is most simply and most solemnly expressed. At one level the material elements of bread and wine are offered to God. At another and deeper level these physical elements represent the body and blood of Christ. Physical matter was the vehicle that God used to express his own being to us. In sharing the elements and celebrating the Eucharist we are linking ourselves to the mysterious sacrifice that Christ made for the entire world. We are also offering the whole realm of nature up to God.

Jesus was both the High Priest and the sacrificial victim. In stressing our own role as priests we must not forget that we too are victims. Perhaps just as important as our responsibility to articulate the prayers of the dumb animals and inanimate elements is our role as fellow-sufferers with the threatened rain forests and the species doomed to extinction. The principle of sacrifice is fundamental to all life, human and non-human. We stand together with the rest of creation, groaning and in travail, as we look forward to the liberation and harmony that will come when God's purposes are finally fulfilled. Eastern religions have been better than Christianity at expressing the sense of solidarity and holism that should follow from the realisation of this fact. They see humans much more as nature's companions than its masters. When Mount Everest was climbed in 1953 the headlines in western papers arrogantly proclaimed 'Man conquers highest mountain'. Eastern newspapers spoke in terms of 'Man making friends with the mountains'. Christians badly need to recover that sense of solidarity and oneness with nature which was once so strong a feature of our faith.

Of course all things in the natural world are not bright and beautiful any more than they are in the sphere of human relations. The life of both man and nature is shot through with tragedy, cruelty and violence. That is part of the ambiguity and fragility of our physical condition, an aspect of the immaturity and imperfection that waits its completion in the coming of God's kingdom when Christ will be all in all. We do not know how that consummation is to be achieved, whether through the gradual perfection or the sudden transformation of the present order, the creation of a new heaven and a new earth, or through the processes of resurrection and rebirth. What we do know is that the rescuing of nature from its frustration and suffering is closely related to our own human redemption. By working with nature rather than exploiting it, by treating it with reverence and awe rather than arrogant contempt, but expressing its groans and its prayers in words and symbols, we are helping that mysterious process of cosmic redemption whereby the earth shall be filled with the knowledge of the Lord as the waters cover the sea.

Postscript
Some practical suggestions
for greening the churches

I am conscious that so far the tone of this book has been predominantly theological and theoretical. This seems to me to be the essential starting point for making Christianity environment-friendly once again. Until we come to a realisation that God is Green, that he is deeply concerned for the whole of his creation and calls us to share that concern, little is likely to happen in the way of practical action or constructive dialogue with those outside our faith who are also concerned about the environment.

But Christianity is about worship and action in the world as well as thinking about God and his purposes for creation. What can churches and congregations do to express the kind of faith which has been discussed in this book and which I profoundly hope more and more Christians will come to rediscover in their own way and in accordance with their own traditions? In these concluding pages I offer some practical suggestions, although they simply scratch the surface and are more in the nature of preliminary jottings than a comprehensive agenda for future action. This is an area on which more work needs to be done, indeed there are many people who are presently applying themselves to it.

Public worship is an obvious starting place for churches to express the essential greenness of the Christian faith. The annual harvest festival springs to mind as an appropriate time to consider the human relationship with nature. For most congregations it is the one occasion in the year when, as well as displays of flowers, the fruits of nature are brought into the church and provide a focal point for worship. Not long ago, in keeping with the mentality that still prevails in much of the agricultural industry, harvest festivals came near to becoming celebrations of intensive high-input farming with all its disastrous environmental effects. A particularly ghastly up-dated version of one of best-loved harvest hymns is still, I regret to say, to be heard in some churches even though it spreads the gospel of pollution:

> We plough the fields with tractors,
>   With drills we sow the land;
> But growth is still the wondrous gift
>   Of God's almighty hand.
> We add the fertilizers
>   To help the growing grain,
> But for its full fruition
>   Its needs God's sun and rain.

To me those lines seem all too reminiscent of John Betjeman's parody of 'We plough the field and scatter' which begins:

> We spray the fields and scatter
>   The poison on the ground
> So that no wicked flowers
>   Upon our farm be found.
> We like whatever helps us
>   To line our purse with pence;
> The twenty-four hour broiler-house
>   And neat electric fence.

However over recent years there has been a welcome shift in the emphasis of many harvest festival services away from thanksgiving for agricultural over-production and towards an expression of concern about the environment and a consideration of the growing gap between the world's haves and have-nots. Much useful material is being produced for use with children, notably by Christian Aid which has issued free leaflets exploring such issues as the destruction of the Brazilian rain forest, the dumping of nuclear waste and industrial pollution, with worship suggestions on the back. A number of new hymns have been written in the past few years with a strong ecological message particularly suitable for singing at harvest festivals. They include Doris Whitney's 'Oh God of all creation', Father James Quinn's 'The seed is Christ's, the harvest his' (translated and adapted from an original Celtic verse) and Fred Pratt Green's 'God in his love for us lent us this planet', which ends with the admirable sentiment:

> Earth is the Lord's: it is ours to enjoy it,
> Ours, as his stewards, to farm and defend.
> From its pollution, misuse and destruction,
> Good Lord, deliver us, world without end!

Hymnody both new and old is an important resource for expressing the greenness of our faith. At the end of Chapter 4 I quoted from some sadly neglected or expurgated older hymns which speak of the cosmic dimension of Christ. There are other well-loved traditional hymns that also express well the Green heart of Christianity: 'For the beauty of the earth'; 'All creatures of our God and king'; 'There is a book who runs may read'; 'The spacious firmament on high'; and not least that grand old favourite, 'Immortal, invisible, God only wise', which is now seldom sung but which comes close to panentheism in its third verse:

> To all, life Thou givest – to both great and small;
> In all life Thou livest, the true life of all;
> We blossom and flourish as leaves on the tree,
> And wither and perish – but nought changeth Thee.

Among more modern hymns which could add a welcome Green tone to regular Sunday worship are the verses by Albert Bayly which begin:

> Lord of the boundless curves of space
> and time's deep mystery,
> To your creative might we trace
> all nature's energy.

Fred Kaan has also written a good Green hymn which begins:

God gave us as in trust to hold
Creation and its wealth untold,
But we have with uncaring hand
Destroyed its green and raped the land.

It would be good to see normal Sunday services enlivened by
some of the themes and the objects from nature which nor-
mally only get introduced into churches once a year at harvest
festival time. We could usefully take a tip from Orthodox
churches which are regularly decorated with foliage for other
major Christian festivals. There is surely room for a spring
service which explores through Christian eyes the themes of
growth and rebirth as they apply both to humans and the
natural world. A number of old traditions associated with
celebrating the fertility and beauty of nature could surely be
revived without allegations of incipient paganism. One which
is, thankfully, very much alive and well is the practice of well-
dressing in Derbyshire, which involves the Church visibly
celebrating the goodness of God's creation. Similar services
blessing springs, wells and other natural features could perhaps be held in other parts of the country. They would have
the great advantage of taking worship away from the confines
of ecclesiastical buildings and into the world outside. Indeed
the practice of holding outdoor services is another old tradition which we would do well revive – apart from anything
else if we are to have hotter summers because of the greenhouse effect, we might as well make the most of them!

Churches can also be effective witnesses to God's continuing concern for his creation by setting an example of good
environmental practice to the communities of which they are
part. I know of several large urban churches which collect
waste paper for recycling, raising funds while at the same
time demonstrating their ecological awareness. This kind of
activity might usefully be extended to cover other categories
of household waste. There has been some controversy in
recent years about churchyards, and specifically as to whether
they should be kept neatly mown or left in a semi-wild state
to encourage wild flowers and butterflies. Possibly some kind
of compromise is desirable which prevents an appearance of

total neglect and disorder while at the same time preserving an area which can be a valuable habitat for wildlife. In rural areas the Church can act as a forum to bring together farmers, conservationists, local residents and others interested in the local environment. Perhaps the major national churches could demonstrate a direct pastoral concern for the earth and all that is within it by appointing chaplains to the countryside as well as to industry.

There is one particular area where the Church as an institution can have a direct impact on the environment and where it can also act as a pioneer for change. Britain's two established churches are landowners on a significant scale. The Church of England, through the Church Commissioners, owns over 160,000 acres of agricultural land currently valued at around £150 million. In addition individual diocesan boards of finance own and administer glebe properties covering around 100,000 acres and yielding an annual income of over £9 million. On a much smaller scale, the General Trustees of the Church of Scotland administer more than 700 glebes, each of which consists of several acres of good agricultural land.

At present the policy of the bodies which administer these church lands is to maximise the revenue from them which goes towards paying stipends for clergy and other necessary expenses. Indeed there is a legal obligation on them to do so. This is understandable but it is having a number of unfortunate consequences. The Church of England in particular is selling off much of its land to developers. This can clash directly with the interests both of conservation and local employment. A particularly well-publicised case has arisen in Durham where the Diocesan Board of Finance has received an offer of over £3 million from a major property developer for an area of glebe land in the shadow of the cathedral which is presently occupied by eighty-two allotments. There has been local outrage at the prospect of housing being built on this land and the loss of the allotments.

Should not our two national churches be thinking of how their role as landlords can be fitted into a theological understanding of the earth as belonging to God and to be treated with respect and dignity by the humans who hold it on trust. At present the great majority of the land holdings of both the Church of England and the Church of Scotland are rented out to large farmers. We know that there is already too much land under intensive cultivation in Britain, indeed the government is paying farmers to set land aside and leave it fallow. Could not the churches make over at least a part of their substantial land holdings either for conservation areas or for organic smallholdings and allotments for the unemployed?

A lead has been taken in this area by the Lutheran Church in the Nordelbe region of Schleswig-Holstein in West Germany. In 1982 it adopted new guidelines for the management of church-owned land which stressed social and ecological factors as well as the economic requirement. When new tenancy agreements are concluded they must secure non-intensive agricultural use of church-owned land. The guidelines lay down that no chemical fertilisers or pesticides should be used on the edge of fields, that fields should be left fallow for a year or two and that non-intensive cropping should be practised. They also suggest that churchyards should become ecological retreats which are seen in theological terms as 'gardens of life'. One of the Lutheran pastors in the region, who serves as the church's ecology officer, notes that 'The aim is still to achieve the best possible return, by honouring the land as God's creation as well as the farmer who is God's co-worker.'

It seems to me that one of the most constructive things that the main churches in Britain could do with their land is to divide it into smallholdings and allotments to be worked organically by local people who lack land and capital and are keen to grow crops either for themselves or for cash. In doing this the Church would in fact be reverting to a very old tradition. In Victorian times it was quite common for clergymen to help the poor in their parish by finding them allotments, often on the glebe. Even in urban areas there may well be small areas of land adjacent to churchyards and in sprawling vicarage gardens which can be used for organic market-gardening or developed as wildlife habitats. In Dundee the Scottish Episcopal Church has established a highly successful garden project which is based on a churchyard and adjoining rectory garden and which trains unemployed people in basic horticultural skills. The project has spread to include growing flowers and vegetables in the gardens of institutions such as old people's homes and children's homes.

There is an even simpler way the Church can make a positive contribution to the environment and put the Green gospel into practice. Nearly every church has a garden or lawn around it or at least a yard or path which separates it from the street. One or two trees planted in this space add to the beauty of the neighbourhood as well as making a theological statement. When a tree was planted in the garden of Fulwood Chapel in Sheffield in 1987 in memory of a former chapel secretary and trustee, the Revd Francis Simons, a Unitarian minister, wrote a poem which seems to me to express very well how much such an apparently small and simple gesture can mean. I quote it with his permission:

To plant a tree is to say Yes to life:
It is to affirm our faith in the future.

To plant a tree is to acknowledge our debt to the past:
Seeds are not created out of nothing.

To plant a tree is to co-operate in Nature's work
Whereby all forms of life are interdependent.

To plant a tree is a token of sorrow for past mistakes:
When we took life's gifts for granted.

To plant a tree is to make a social statement
For green-consciousness, for conservation and ecology.

To plant a tree is to enhance the quality of life:
It brings beauty to the eyes and uplift to the spirit.

To plant a tree is to make a spiritual point:
We are all members of the Tree of Life, we stand or fall
together.

Notes

INTRODUCTION (pp. 1–11)

1 *Science*, vol. 155, no. 3767 (10 March 1967), pp. 1204–7.
2 *New Scientist*, vol. 48, no. 732 (31 December 1970), p. 575.
3 C. Westermann, *Creation*, tr. J. Scullion (SPCK, London, 1974), p. 3.
4 H. Montefiore, ed., *Man and Nature* (Collins, London, 1975), p. 13.
5 *Church and Society Newsletter*, no. 7 (September 1987).
6 Teilhard de Chardin, *Hymn of the Universe*, tr. S. Bartholomew (Collins, London, 1965), p. 61.
7 *The Times*, 3 June 1989.

CHAPTER 1 (pp. 12–32)

1 J. Calvin, *Commentaries on the First Book of Moses, called Genesis*, tr. J. King (London, 1847), vol. I, p. 96.
2 Quoted in K. V. Thomas, *Man and the Natural World* (Allen Lane, London, 1983), p. 20.
3 Quoted in *While the Earth Endures* (Church of Scotland, Edinburgh, 1986), p. 4.
4 *Observer*, 13 October 1963.
5 Quoted in K. V. Thomas, op. cit. p. 151.
6 Quoted in C. Birch and J. B. Cobb, *The Liberation of Life: from cell to community* (Cambridge, 1981), p. 147.
7 W. S. Blunt, *My Diaries* (Martin Secker, London, 1932), p. 343.
8 C. Westermann, *Genesis 1–11: a commentary* (SPCK, London, 1984), p. 159.

9   J. E. Lovelock, *Gaia: a new look at life on earth* (Oxford, 1979), p. 9.
10 H. Montefiore, ed., op. cit. p. 88.
11 ibid. pp. 96–7.
12 E. Echlin, 'The Holocaust of Leviathan', *America* (15 October 1988), p. 257.
13 Quoted in A. R. Peacocke, *The Sciences and Theology in the Twentieth Century* (Clarendon Press, Oxford, 1982), p. 150.
14 Quoted in S. McDonagh, *To Care for the Earth* (Cassell, London, 1986), p. 46.
15 C. Westermann, *Creation*, p. 176.

CHAPTER 2 (pp. 33–51)

1   *Science*, op. cit. p. 1205.
2   R. H. Fuller, *Interpreting the Miracles* (SCM, London, 1963), p. 9.
3   W. Temple, *Readings in St John's Gospel* (Macmillan, London, 1959), pp. xx-xxi.
4   Y. Feliks, *Nature and Man in the Bible* (Soncino Press, London, 1981), p. ix.
5   G. S. Hendry, *Theology of Nature* (Westminster Press, Philadelphia, 1980), pp. 20–1.
6   Quoted in Lord Longford, *Life of St Francis of Assisi* (Weidenfeld & Nicolson, London, 1978), p. 76.)
7   A. R. Peacocke, *Creation and the World of Science* (Clarendon Press, Oxford, 1979), p. 105.
8   Quoted in G. S. Hendry, op. cit. pp. 63–4.
9   Quoted in P. Gregorios, *The Human Presence* (World Council of Churches, Geneva, 1977), p. 31.
10 J. Polkinghorne, *One World: the interaction of science and theology* (SPCK, London, 1986), p. 81.
11 D. Mackay, *Science, Chance and Providence* (Oxford University Press, 1978), p. 5.
12 P. Evdokimov, 'Nature', *Scottish Journal of Theology*, vol. 18, no. 1 (March 1965), p. 5.
13 Teilhard de Chardin, op. cit. p. 70.

CHAPTER 3 (pp. 52–73)

1   B. Willey, *The Seventeenth-Century Background* (Penguin, London, 1964), p. 35.
2   G. S. Hendry, op. cit. p. 55.
3   W. Dantine 'Creation and Redemption', *Scottish Journal of Theology*, vol. 18, no. 2 (1965), p. 140.
4   Quoted in S. McDonagh, op. cit. p. 134.
5   George F. MacLeod, *The Whole Earth Shall Cry Glory: Iona prayers* (Wild Goose Pubns, Iona, 1985), p. 8. Reproduced with permission.
6   B. Anderson, ed., *Creation in the Old Testament* (SPCK, London, 1984), p. 163.
7   J. Calvin, *Institutes of the Christian Religion*, ed. J. T. McNeill (SCM, London, 1961), p. 246.
8   G. H. Sabine, ed., *The Collected Works of Gerrard Winstanley* (Cornell University Press, 1941), p. 204.
9   P. Evdokimov, op. cit. pp. 1, 4.
10 C. F. D. Moule, *Man and Nature in the New Testament* (Athlone Press, London, 1964), p. 20.
11 A. Farrer, *Love Almighty and Ills Unlimited* (Doubleday, New York, 1961), p. 50.
12 J. Moltmann, *The Future of Creation* (SCM, London, 1979), p. 119.
13 C. F. Mooney, *Teilhard de Chardin and the Mystery of Christ* (Collins, London, 1965), p. 31.
14 C. Birch and J. Cobb, op. cit. p. 119.
15 ibid. p. 120.
16 J. Polkinghorne, *Science and Providence* (SPCK, 1989), p. 66.
17 O. Kaiser, *Isaiah 1–12: a commentary* (SCM, 1983), p. 259.
18 F. D. Maurice, *The Doctrine of Sacrifice* (Cambridge, 1854), p. 44.
19 C. Gore, *St Paul's Epistle to the Romans* (Murray, London, 1899), vol. I, p. 305.
20 C. E. B. Cranfield, *A Critical and Exegetical Commentary on the Epistle to the Romans* (T. & T. Clark, Edinburgh, 1975), vol. I, p. 412.
21 C. H. Dodd, *The Meaning of Paul for Today* (Fontana, London, 1958), p. 61.
22 C. Gore, op. cit. p. 303.
23 H. Montefiore, ed., op. cit. p. 31.

CHAPTER 4 (pp. 74–89)

1 Quoted in Mary Midgley, *Beast and Man* (Harvester Press, Hassocks, 1978), p. 219.
2 Quoted in K. V. Thomas, op. cit. p. 140.
3 G. Matheson, 'The Empire of Jesus' in *Rests by the River* (Hodder & Stoughton, London, 1906), p. 13.
4 C. H. Dodd, *The Parables of the Kingdom* (Nisbet, London, 1935), p. 21.
5 See, for example, S. Terrein, *The Elusive Presence* (Harper and Row, 1978).
6 Quoted in K. V. Thomas, op. cit. p. 139.
7 *Revelations of Divine Love Recorded by Julian, Anchoress of Norwich*, ed. Grace Warrack (Methuen, London, 1945), pp. 40–1.
8 G. H. Sabine, ed., op. cit. pp. 113, 117.
9 George F. MacLeod, *Only One Way Left* (Iona Community, Glasgow, 1956), p. 31.
10 Quoted in F. W. Dillistone, *The Christian Understanding of Atonement* (SCM, London, 1984), pp. 74–5.
11 Quoted in P. Evdokimov, op. cit. p. 11.
12 G. S. Hendry, op. cit. p. 216.
13 Quoted in R. Faricy, *Wind and Sea Obey Him* (SCM, London, 1982), p. 73.
14 G. H. Sabine, ed., op. cit. p. 164.
15 C. F. Mooney, op. cit. p. 31; J. Cobb, *Christ in a Pluralistic Age* (Westminster Press, Philadelphia, 1975), p. 76.
16 P. Evdokimov, op. cit. p. 15.
17 Quoted in E. H. Cousins, ed., *Process Theology* (Newman Press, New York, 1971), p. 252.
18 ibid. p. 254.
19 C. F. Mooney, op. cit. pp. 140, 136.
20 N. Beryaev, *Freedom and the Spirit* (Bles, London, 1935), p. 179.
21 P. Evdokimov, op. cit. p. 16.

CHAPTER 5 (pp. 90–106)

1 M. Hale, *The Primitive Origination of Mankind* (London, 1677), p. 370.
2 Quoted in K. V. Thomas, op. cit. p. 155.
3 George F. MacLeod, *Only One Way Left*, pp. 29–30.
4 Quoted in K. V. Thomas, op. cit. p. 255.

5 ibid. p. 237.
6 G. H. Sabine, ed., op. cit. p. 428.
7 Quoted in M. Fox, *Original Blessing* (Bear & Co., New Mexico, 1983), p. 192.
8 P. Gregorios, op. cit. p. 84.
9 Quoted in V. Lossky, *The Mystical Theology of the Eastern Church* (James Clarke, London, 1957), pp. 110–11.
10 Quoted in H. Waddell, *Beasts and Saints* (Constable, London, 1934), p. 136.
11 *Adamnan's Life of Columba* ed. A. O. and M. O. Anderson (Nelson, London, 1961), pp. 313–14.
12 Bonaventura, *Life of St Francis* (SPCK Classics of Western Spirituality, London, 1978), p. 251.
13 G. Matheson, *Searchings in the Silence* (Cassell, London, 1895), pp. 215–16.
14 P. Gregorios, op. cit. p. 80.
15 Bonaventura, *The Soul's Journey to God* (SPCK Classics of Western Spirituality, London, 1978), p. 77.
16 H. Hesse, *Peter Camenzind*, tr. W. J. Strachan (Penguin, London, 1973), pp. 82–3.
17 Quoted in G. S. Hendry, op. cit. p. 56.
18 *Church and Society Newsletter*, no. 7 (September 1987).
19 C. H. Dodd, *The Meaning of Paul for Today* op. cit. p. 33.
20 Quoted in ibid. pp. 33–4.
21 Quoted in P. Gregorios, op. cit. p. 81.
22 A. R. Peacocke, *Creation and the World of Science*, p. 296.
23 H. Montefiore, 'Man and nature: a theological assessment', *Zygon*, no. 12 (1977), p. 206.
24 H. Montefiore, ed., *Man and Nature* (1975), p. 119.